ELLIS OF LEICESTER

A Quaker Family's Vocation

ELLIS OF LEICESTER

A Quaker Family's Vocation

ANDREW MOORE

Laurel House Publishing

First published in 2003

British Library Cataloguing in Publication Data
A catalogue record for this book is available
from the British Library.

ISBN 0 9533628 1 7

Front cover, main picture -
*An engraving from the original portrait of John Ellis which was
presented to him by the Midland Railway in 1858. A portal of
Glenfield tunnel on the Leicester & Swannington Railway (a line
over which he had great influence in its instigation) can be seen
in the background. Further details of the portrait are in appendix II.*
Other pictures -
Joseph Ellis depot at Highgate Wharf, Birmingham in 1899.
Belgrave Hall from the rear gardens.
A John Ellis & Sons lorry loaded with spun concrete pipes.
Typical railway wagon livery from the Ellis & Everard granite quarries.
Sign from Ellis Park, Oadby.

Designed and printed by Laburnum Graphics Ltd.,
Brentwood Road, Leicester. LE2 6AD

Published by Laurel House Publishing,
8 Tennyson Street, Narborough, Leicester LE19 3FD

CONTENTS

PREFACE

Various Ellis names regularly appear when reading about Leicester's history. John Ellis and Edward Shipley Ellis, both of railway fame, Joseph Ellis of Ellis & Everard Ltd, and the seven Ellis sisters of *Belgrave Hall* are just a few, and it was a curiosity at the possible relationship between these names that was the start of this book. Not only was it soon established that they were from the same large Quaker family, but also that they had led far more meritorious and interesting lives than was at first known.

What became apparent was the business enterprise and tremendous public service to Leicester shown by many members of the family, especially during the second half of the nineteenth century, and for these attributes alone the Ellises should be more widely known. This volume is an attempt to do just that.

Other local families have been involved in as many diverse industries as the Ellises, and excelled in service to the community (typical of many Victorian entrepreneurs conscious of their position in society) — the Gimsons, Everards, Pagets and Goddards are examples — and some local family concerns have been more nationally known such as Currys, Halfords and many shoe retailers.[1] However, the Ellises are set apart because so many generations, spanning more than a century and a half, have been involved with a variety of such things as railway management, education, charities, finance, local and national government — as well as their own commercial concerns.

Like most of their self-made, business contemporaries during the expansion of industrial Leicester, the Ellises were Liberal Non-Conformists who helped shape the fortunes of the town following the reforms of local government in the 1830s.[2] Their own particular religion helped their standing in society, the Quakers being renowned for their influence in the business and social world beyond their numbers. All this achieved through living by their principles of fairness and truth, peace, equality, simplicity and a need for social welfare to which it seems they adhered, promoted through their unique system of weekly and monthly 'meetings'.

The book has taken the form of short biographical accounts of the lives of the family members most associated with Leicester — some naturally more detailed than others because of the lives they led — and as part of their achievements, accounts of their business enterprises are included.

A myth surrounds one enterprise, however, that must be clarified. This is that the family had started coalmines near to Nailstone and Bagworth in north-west Leicestershire and built cottages for the workers which grew to become a village called Ellistown. This was, in fact, the work of a landowner from London called Colonel Joseph Joel Ellis who was completely unrelated. Coincidently, the Leicester Ellises did open collieries, but they were at Hucknall in Nottinghamshire. Clarification is also needed regarding a Leicester family that ran worsted spinning and hosiery businesses under the names of G.Ellis and F.Ellis, and had factories in Chancery Street, Newarke Street and Evington Valley Road.[3] They also were unrelated, although, coincidently, some of the Leicester Quaker Ellises were at one time involved in the same trades.

Presenting such a large family can be complicated and so for clarity the book has been divided into four sections to detail the four central characters — the brothers JOHN, JOSEPH, JAMES and ROBERT — and their main descendants. For ease of reference, these family members are shown on simplified family trees at the beginning of the book and at the start of sections 1 and 2. (A more detailed chart is in appendix I.) Reference to local place names can be made in appendix VI.

Much of the information for the book has been obtained from the Record Office for Leicestershire, Leicester and Rutland, and special thanks go to members of the staff there who were always extremely helpful. A debt is also owed to the Ellises themselves for recording parts of their own history. Valuable information has been readily available from their privately-produced publications details of which appear in the bibliography. Special acknowledgement goes to Joan Johnson for her book about one of the four brothers, James Ellis, and his great work in Ireland; also to Rita Eaton for her writing about Belgrave and John Ellis's seven daughters who resided there.

The help is much appreciated of Bob Geary of Ellis & Everard plc, Bradford for unearthing historical information about that company and the availability of company photographs, also of the staff at Lafarge Aggregates Limited, Mountsorrel, where information regarding the John Ellis company was obtained. For supplying other information, checking draft text and technical help my grateful thanks go to Ellis family members Elizabeth Hall, Charlotte Ellis and Katherine Slay, and to Rikie Ford, Edward Moore, Hilary Leigh-Browne, Paul Quibell, and Richard Moore to whom I am very much indebted.

(Photographs referenced LMARS have been reproduced by kind permission of the Leicestershire Museums, Arts and Records Service.)

Andrew Moore 2003

ELLIS FAMILY TREE — ABRIDGED

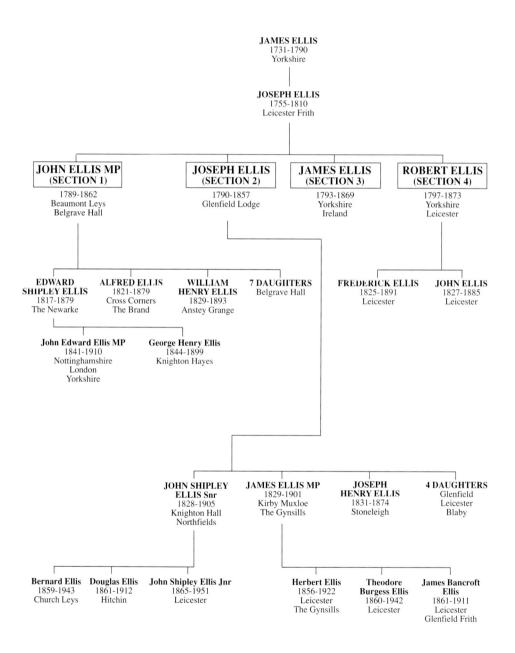

JAMES ELLIS
1731-1790
Yorkshire

JOSEPH ELLIS
1755-1810
Leicester Frith

JOHN ELLIS MP
(SECTION 1)
1789-1862
Beaumont Leys
Belgrave Hall

JOSEPH ELLIS
(SECTION 2)
1790-1857
Glenfield Lodge

JAMES ELLIS
(SECTION 3)
1793-1869
Yorkshire
Ireland

ROBERT ELLIS
(SECTION 4)
1797-1873
Yorkshire
Leicester

EDWARD
SHIPLEY ELLIS
1817-1879
The Newarke

ALFRED ELLIS
1821-1879
Cross Corners
The Brand

WILLIAM
HENRY ELLIS
1829-1893
Anstey Grange

7 DAUGHTERS
Belgrave Hall

FREDERICK ELLIS
1825-1891
Leicester

JOHN ELLIS
1827-1885
Leicester

John Edward Ellis MP
1841-1910
Nottinghamshire
London
Yorkshire

George Henry Ellis
1844-1899
Knighton Hayes

JOHN SHIPLEY
ELLIS Snr
1828-1905
Knighton Hall
Northfields

JAMES ELLIS MP
1829-1901
Kirby Muxloe
The Gynsills

JOSEPH
HENRY ELLIS
1831-1874
Stoneleigh

4 DAUGHTERS
Glenfield
Leicester
Blaby

Bernard Ellis
1859-1943
Church Leys

Douglas Ellis
1861-1912
Hitchin

John Shipley Ellis Jnr
1865-1951
Leicester

Herbert Ellis
1856-1922
Leicester
The Gynsills

Theodore
Burgess Ellis
1860-1942
Leicester

James Bancroft
Ellis
1861-1911
Leicester
Glenfield Frith

INTRODUCTION

THE ELLISES ARRIVE IN LEICESTERSHIRE

The immediate forebears of the section of the Ellis family that was so prominent in Leicestershire in the nineteenth and twentieth centuries emanate from South Yorkshire.[4] They were members of the Society of Friends (Quakers), a religion that had spread particularly to the northern counties since George Fox, a Leicestershire Puritan from Fenny Drayton, had founded the movement around the year 1650.

The Yorkshire Ellises were primarily farmers and one member of the family, James, moved around 1750 to start his own farm at Beighton near the Derbyshire border. Here, he married Leicestershire-born Anne Shipley (although her family was from Staffordshire) with whom he had seven children before her death in 1779. Three years later James decided to move again, this time to Leicestershire with just one of his children, Joseph. They arrived in the county with Joseph having to wheel not only the family furniture in a wagon but also his father who was by then an invalid. Exactly why they moved is uncertain, but possibly it was to be near two sets of relatives. These were the Shipleys (whose associations were to be reflected in many of the Ellis family forenames) and also a large family of fellow Quakers — the Burgesses.[5]

James and Joseph leased a farm on the *Sharman's Lodge* estate in Leicester Frith — an area near to Groby Road where Glenfield Hospital now stands. Much to the consternation of the Quaker fraternity (although it was approved by both families) Joseph married his cousin, Rebecca Burgess of Wigston, in 1788. This was two years before his father died.

Joseph and Rebecca had six children at *Sharman's Lodge* between 1789 and 1797. The first-born was JOHN, who was destined to become the most celebrated of all the local Ellis family, and he was followed by JOSEPH, JAMES, Anne, William (who died in infancy) and ROBERT. The children grew up on the farm, except when John, Joseph and James were boarding at schools in Tamworth and Hartshill, travelling there by alternating rides on the family donkey. When there were sufficient mature hands, in 1807 the family also leased an adjoining farm about one mile away at Beaumont Leys. The eldest son, John, then 18, took on the running of this farm.

The Beaumont Leys estate was large — about 900 acres — on which the Ellises were tenants of the old manor house and about 370 acres. Another main dwelling on the estate was *Beaumont Lodge*, occupied and farmed by members of the related Burgess family.

In 1810 Joseph (senior) died after a very profitable life farming. An existing account book that he started in 1804 shows meticulously his purchases and products of the two farms[6] which included oats, barley, wheat, flour (milled at Anstey and Belgrave water mills), cattle (some driven to London by road for sale), sheep, cheese, wool, pigs, potatoes and blue and white (!) peas. At the time of his death, Joseph (senior) had retired to Leicester and left John to continue running the farm at Beaumont Leys, and left *Sharman's Lodge* — then a farm of about 250 acres — in the hands of his second son Joseph. The third and fourth sons, James and Robert, left to start separate lives in Yorkshire, the county where many family acquaintances remained.

SECTION 1
JOHN ELLIS - HIS DESCENDANTS AND COMPANIES

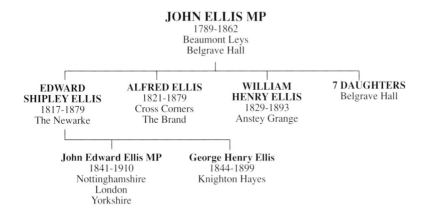

JOHN ELLIS MP
1789-1862
Beaumont Leys
Belgrave Hall

EDWARD SHIPLEY ELLIS
1817-1879
The Newarke

ALFRED ELLIS
1821-1879
Cross Corners
The Brand

WILLIAM HENRY ELLIS
1829-1893
Anstey Grange

7 DAUGHTERS
Belgrave Hall

John Edward Ellis MP
1841-1910
Nottinghamshire
London
Yorkshire

George Henry Ellis
1844-1899
Knighton Hayes

JOHN ELLIS MP
1789-1862

Following his schooling days, John Ellis led an amazingly successful life. He firstly became a very proficient farmer at Beaumont Leys, continuing the detailed accounts that his father had started and was always able to do his share of the ploughing, reaping, milking and so on throughout his farming life. He was even adept at 'straw draining' having learnt the craft as a boy when staying on an Essex farm.[7] He contributed to the improvement of the breed of shorthorn cattle, became a respected judge at agricultural shows and in 1836 gave evidence before a Parliamentary select committee on distress due to the state of agriculture in rural districts. By 1836 his farm comprised 150 acres of arable land, 250 acres for grazing and an orchard containing almost every variety of native fruit tree.

He was married in 1816 to Martha Shipley, daughter of John Shipley of

John Ellis, 1789-1862, of Beaumont Leys and Belgrave Hall. (LMARS)

Priscilla, second wife of John Ellis. (LMARS)

Uttoxeter, but was married for only one year as she died soon after a son, Edward Shipley Ellis, was born in 1817. John married again in 1820 to Priscilla Evans by whom he had three sons and seven daughters, all born at Beaumont Leys between 1821 and 1839.

During this time he had started his business career with brother, Joseph, and they are shown in a trade directory for the first time in 1827 as corn dealers and maltsters of St Nicholas Street, Leicester, moving to Sanvey Gate the following year.

1828 marked a significant point in John Ellis's life for it was the beginning of his deep involvement in railway management. In October of that year he was approached by a William Stenson, who asked for John's assistance in promoting a railway to bring coal into Leicester from the North West Leicestershire collieries, including Stenson's recently opened mine at Whitwick.[8] This would help undercut the price of coal in Leicester that was arriving by canal at West Bridge wharf mainly from Nottinghamshire and Derbyshire.

At this time talk about the revolutionary new railways was rife due to the successful opening of the Stockton & Darlington line in 1825 and the current building of the Liverpool & Manchester railway. Quaker, Edward Pease, had promoted the Stockton & Darlington to reduce coal prices for the benefit of the local populace as much as for local business and his own pocket[9] — in true Quaker philanthropic fashion — and quite possibly John Ellis would have had a similar idea for Leicester.

To check the viability of the Leicestershire line Ellis agreed with Stenson to approach George Stephenson who had engineered the Stockton & Darlington and was currently working on the Liverpool & Manchester line. Ellis already knew Stephenson well through another Quaker, James Cropper, a shipping merchant who was co-promoter of the Liverpool & Manchester line and, significantly, was the uncle of Ellis's second wife. (A consequence of John Ellis's Quaker family ties was that he was, jointly with brother

A 19th century engraving of the house at Beaumont Leys.

A present-day view of Beaumont Leys, now the Home Farm community centre.

Joseph, already financially involved in the attempt at reclaiming the marshland of Chat Moss across which the Liverpool & Manchester was to run.)[10] George Stephenson was enthusiastic about the Leicestershire line and particularly helped with the raising of its finances. However, he was so preoccupied on other new lines he was only able to act as consultant and arranged for his son, Robert, to be engineer on what was to become the Leicester & Swannington Railway.[11]

The railway company was set up with John Ellis and brother, Joseph, as very active directors. Work on the line was started and, after many problems with building a tunnel at Glenfield, the major part of it opened in 1832. During construction, George Stephenson was an occasional guest of John Ellis at Beaumont Leys (as was James Cropper, although probably not at the same time, as Stephenson and Cropper constantly disagreed on the development of the Liverpool & Manchester line). Robert Stephenson is also known to have stayed regularly at Joseph's house in Glenfield village.

John was then, independently of his brother, in business selling the resulting cheaper Leicestershire coal brought down the new line to the terminus at West Bridge. Here he was agent for the Snibston colliery — a mine opened by George and Robert Stephenson near to the present Coalville during their work on the railway. John was a partner in this mine as well as in Stenson's Whitwick colliery.

Joining him in his business enterprise was his eldest son, Edward Shipley Ellis, and in later years, when they had reached maturity, two other sons, Alfred and William Henry also helped run his expanding company. (A further son, Charles, was unfortunately of 'unsound mind' and lived at a home in York.) In addition to West Bridge, coal was later sold at some stations on the Midland Counties Railway — a line running through Loughborough, Leicester and on to Rugby — when opened in 1840. John Ellis's company, John Ellis & Sons, also burnt and sold lime.

Leicester and Swannington Railway.

Soar-Lane Weighing Machine, Leicester.

No. *3*   *Nov 2nd* 184*1*

Name *Pettifor to Ellis*

Residence *Beaumont Leys*

Description *Manure*

	Tons.	Cwt.	Qrs.
Gross	5	16	0
Tare	1	4	0
Nett	4	12	0

Richard Thomas — Weighing Clerk.

A Leicester & Swannington Railway weighbridge ticket dated November 2 1841. It was made out for a delivery of manure by carrier, Pettifor, to Ellis of Beaumont Leys.

As if running the business, the farm, directorship of the Leicester & Swannington and his large family were insufficient, John was also occupied in the affairs of Leicester Borough. He was elected to the Town Council in 1837 and made an Alderman in 1838. Reports say that he refused to be Mayor because he was unable to take the oath, which was against the Quaker doctrine. However, by then the law had been changed to accommodate this religious constraint.

By 1838 he was also working for the Midland Counties Railway of which he was a large shareholder. With his knowledge of farming costs and crop values, the railway employed him to assess compensation payable to farmers affected by the line's construction. Subsequently, he was made a director of the company in 1842 and was the major instigator in its amalgamation with the North Midland and Birmingham & Derby Railways to form the Midland Railway in 1844. This new company had George Hudson, the 'railway king', as chairman and John Ellis was appointed his deputy. By 1845 John's reputation had grown quickly for he was by then also a director of the London & Birmingham, Birmingham & Gloucester and Dunstable Railways and later of the Manchester & Buxton and London & North Western Railways.[12] He was even on the board for a number of years of the Belfast Gas Company.

With mention of the London & Birmingham line, during its construction, a serious accident occurred at Watford tunnel in 1835 due to a sudden fall of sand and gravel, resulting in ten fatalities. The contractors, Copeland & Harding of Leicester (who had encountered similar problems when building Glenfield tunnel) were badly affected financially at the setback and called on John and Joseph Ellis and a Robert Birkley to form a 'co-partnership'.[13] They were able to surmount the problems and reputedly made a reasonable profit on the completed contract.[14]

At the Midland Railway, financial malpractices by George Hudson had caused heavy losses to the shareholders and he was consequently dismissed in 1849. John Ellis was promoted to chairman, a position he held with much acclaim particularly because of the way he managed to steady the ship after Hudson's demise. During his time at the Midland, John was chairman of the Construction Committee and instrumental in enlarging the system both by securing the important Bristol to Birmingham line ahead of the Great Western Railway[15] (and so preventing the continued spread of the incongruous broad gauge system to the midlands) and also by reaching London through building the Leicester & Hitchin line. This line achieved the long-awaited freedom from using London & North Western Railway lines to London south of Rugby.

Ellis terminated his office as chairman in 1857 (although he continued on the Construction Committee) but his successor, George B.Paget, was almost immediately taken ill and died and so Ellis remained in the seat until 1858. The Midland Railway, in recognition of his achievements, presented him with a 1,000 guinea (£1,050) testimonial comprising a huge service of silverware and a full-length portrait by John Lucas of himself standing by the railway in front of Glenfield tunnel.[16] More details of the testimonial are in appendix II.

His farming was given up in 1846 following a disagreement with a new landlord at Beaumont Leys, and he bought a large property at Belgrave near Leicester. (Two of his children, Alfred and Lucy, continued to run the farm at Beaumont Leys until 1849.) The new house became known as *Belgrave Hall* and adjoining the land at the rear he bought another property, a large Georgian house, for his son Alfred's family residence, eventually called *Cross Corners*.

John and his family found a great contrast between the country life and the more urban type of living. They were now closer to the poverty that was prevalent in the 'hungry forties' and the family was very charitable to the desperate villagers and townspeople of Leicester. Typical of John's charity was his providing a local schoolroom in his first year at Belgrave.

During the early years at his new home his interest in politics grew. From fighting local problems he went on to national issues and was chosen as a Liberal Member of Parliament for the Borough of Leicester in 1848. Like many leading Quakers, he had been an outspoken champion of the Anti-Slavery Movement, and in the House was a blunt but sincere and friendly 'character'. It was at this time that he was responsible for taking a fellow board member of the Midland Railway to the Building Committee of the Great Exhibition as a potential designer of the exhibition hall. This was the man eventually trusted with the task, Joseph Paxton.

The grand 'cottage' built by John Ellis at Brand Hill for use as a retreat in 1852, but subsequently replaced.

John relinquished his Parliamentary seat in 1852, due, he said, because of his commitment to the Midland Railway.

Regarding the John Ellis company, which was run mainly by his three sons in his absence on other duties, the core of the business was in merchandising coal and lime, but there were diverse subsidiaries. Land was both rented and purchased at Barrow-on-Soar for the extraction and burning of lime, and between Woodhouse Eaves and Swithland (Brand Hill) in the Charnwood Forest, land was purchased from a William Hind in 1851, some of which contained slate quarries. Slate was extracted, mostly for roofing, and sold through the company depots.[17] In that delightful area John let the cottages he bought with the land, and for his family use, a substantial cottage in 'Swiss-Gothic' style was built of slate in 1852.[18] It was in sylvan surroundings and a place where he loved to retreat. His will shows that he also had a cottage in Oakham and held property at Chat Moss and Beeston (Cheshire). Clearly, he was reasonably well off, and the fact that five of his daughters remained unmarried — usually quite a financial strain on a family — had little significance.

More diverse in his business interests was his involvement in the worsted spinning trade. This was a growing industry in Leicester that was becoming increasingly automated to supply sufficient yarn for the hundreds of stocking frames in the area. John Ellis, with his eldest son, Edward Shipley, saw the business potential.[19] They went into partnership with John Whitmore who had already moved into the industry having once owned a fleet of canal barges and who was already running a factory in the West Bridge area. The new company, Whitmore & Ellis, started in 1844 with the Ellises each holding a quarter share and John Whitmore a half. In

1849 a six-storey factory, especially designed by William Flint, was built for the company by the river on the south side of West Bridge Street. It was then the largest factory in Leicester with the tallest chimney at 165 feet. After about ten years the business traded as John Whitmore & Company, a name that lasted until about 1904 when it was amalgamated with J & J Baldwin & Partners Ltd (later Patons & Baldwins).[20] The building was subsequently owned by H.T.H.Peck Ltd and the Grade II listed building is now occupied by the Land Registry. Although involved in so many fields, on the census return of 1851, John Ellis's occupation was simply shown as 'Worsted Spinner and Member of Parliament'!

On his retirement as the Midland Railway chairman, John became a county magistrate in

A group of Ellis gravestones in the south-west corner of Welford Road cemetery — typically modest Quaker memorials.

1858 and was made a director of Pares's Leicestershire Banking Company. He was also Chairman of the Leicester Savings Bank and a benefactor and governor of the Leicester Infirmary. However, his health was deteriorating and after an illness of several weeks (during which he was still overseeing line construction for the Midland Railway) he died at Belgrave on 26 October 1862. This self-made man, described in his obituary as 'a vigorous mind in a vigorous body', was buried at Welford Road cemetery beneath a simple Quaker headstone (oddly, not made of his own Swithland slate as one might expect). Near him is buried his wife, Priscilla, who survived him by ten years and also the graves of many relations and former business partner, John Whitmore. Known family graves in Leicester are shown in appendix V.

The house at Beaumont Leys where he lived for 40 years can still be seen, although surrounded by houses and shops rather than the masses of oaks, limes and elms as in Ellis's day. The three-storey, gabled building, built c.1649 and listed Grade II, is now used as a Neighbourhood Centre at the Home Farm complex on Strasbourg Drive. (*Beaumont Lodge*, once the home of the Burgesses, also remains on the same estate in use as a Training and Community Centre.)

The John Ellis name is remembered near to his home at Belgrave by the naming of Ellis Avenue and subsequently the schools on that road. The senior schools were superseded by the John Ellis College, once situated across the river in Corporation Road.

EDWARD SHIPLEY ELLIS 1817-1879

John Ellis's eldest son, Edward, was brought up on the farm at Beaumont Leys with his stepmother and ten half-brothers and sisters. He, no doubt, joined in with them to do his fair share on the farm, but at the start of his working life, rather than farming, decided to join his father in merchandising coal and lime. He also worked in the worsted spinning trade joining the family partnership in the Whitmore & Ellis Company.

In 1838 he married Emma Burgess (from the same family as his grandmother) who he first met when attending the opening of the Leicester & Swannington Railway with his father at the age of 15. After their marriage they lived in a large, seventeenth century house opposite the Trinity Hospital in The Newarke, Leicester. It was owned by the Burgess family and was so large it was divided into two properties. It stood in walled grounds

Edward Shipley Ellis, 1817-1879, of The Newarke. (LMARS)

containing lawns, orchard and elm trees and extended at the rear to Richmond Street. Edward Shipley purchased the property in 1853.[21] In 1841 a son, John Edward, was born (followed by George Henry, Emily and Sydney) and the next year saw the start of Edward's long life in public service. In this, and with his business career, eventual involvement with railway management and landownership, his life followed a similar pattern to that of his father.

In public service, he became a Leicester councillor in 1842 and was subsequently elected almost continuously until 1861. He was Mayor in 1860, Alderman between 1861 and 1873 and from 1862 a borough and then county magistrate. He was on the Board of Guardians — administering poor relief on behalf of the council — and at one time its chairman. He was also chairman of the Leicester Waterworks Company and involved with the Museums, Free Library, School of Art and Vaughan Working Men's College. There was also time to be president of the Leicester Liberal Association and vice chairman of the Governors of Wyggeston Hospital Boys' and Girls' Schools which he helped instigate in 1877-8. (His daughter, Emily, was a manager at the Girls' School.) Edward was also auditor for both the Leicester Infirmary and Leicester Gas Company.

Rather than wait for others to get things done he would often take the necessary steps himself. This was shown when he found that the master sweeps of Leicester were not adhering to the Chimney Sweeps Act, and so he bought them all patent sweeping brushes and warned them that if they continued to send boys up chimneys, as a magistrate, he would

The home of Edward Shipley Ellis in The Newarke, Leicester. The site is now occupied by the Hawthorne Building of De Montfort University.

prosecute them.[22] He also gave £1,100 to the museum to build a lecture room and art school, but perhaps the most public-spirited act of all was his paying most of the costs to remove six feet from the top of a very steep hill near Welford Road cemetery to ease the burden of draft-horses. He was a trustee of the Leicester Savings Bank and president of two organisations that became the Leicester Permanent and Leicester Temperance Building Societies. (Eventually they formed part of the Alliance & Leicester Building Society.)

On the industrial side, as well as running the company of John Ellis & Sons, he was the chief instigator of a speculative venture into coal mining. Along with his brother, Alfred, and two other partners, he started a shaft at Hucknall Torkard in Nottinghamshire in March 1861 and coal production started three years later.[23] The Hucknall Colliery Company was founded, initially managed by his eldest son, John Edward. A second pit was sunk nearby in 1866 and the company was successfully run as a family concern until nationalisation in the 1940s.

His first known involvement with railways was in 1846 when he was auditor for the short-lived Dunstable Railway. He was made a director of the Midland Railway in 1857 (whilst his father was chairman) and then became chairman himself from 1873 until his death.[24] There were two notable achievements during Edward's chairmanship. Firstly, against vehement opposition, he allowed third-class passengers on all trains and greatly improved their conditions, thus attracting many more passengers. Soon after, he abolished second-class travel — this policy eventually followed by all of the major railway companies. Secondly, he guided the company through the notoriously difficult and lengthy task of building the Settle and Carlisle Railway over the North Yorkshire and Westmorland fells.

Later in life, he invested heavily in property. Land was purchased, particularly during 1875-6, from six separate landowners (Challis, Salt, Harris, Pares, Crossley and female Ellis cousins) when he acquired most of Glenfield Frith and part of Glenfield totalling approximately 110 acres.[25] The land stretched eastwards from the centre of Glenfield to Leicester Frith on Groby Road and included two sets of buildings — Glenfield Frith farm and

The rear entrance to the Ellis Memorial Technical School, Applegate, now part of Leicester Grammar School.

Glenfield Frith house, the latter standing almost above Glenfield tunnel and was eventually known as *The Cedars*. A small piece of the land was given to the Methodists in Glenfield to replace their chapel and school, the foundation stone of the building being laid by Edward's daughter, Emily, in 1876.

He also held property in Leicester. Included were Spa Gardens on which there were premises between Humberstone Road and Erskine Street, and also property in West Bridge Street which was transferred to the Leicester Coffee & Cocoa House Company in 1877. This was a very successful enterprise he helped set up with fellow members of the Leicester Temperance Society to offer alternative meeting venues for all classes to avoid the 'demon drink'.[26] There were eventually 15 such places established in Leicester at various times, all in very grand buildings.[27]

1877 also saw tragedy when his youngest son, Sydney, a keen geologist and scientist, died having inhaled toxic gasses whilst experimenting with chemical worsted dyes at his home in The Newarke. Two years later the whole community was shocked when Edward, aged 62, also died there after a sudden illness. It had a great effect on many people in Leicester for he had dedicated almost 40 years of his life in their service and was still extremely active. Because of his natural and impartial chairmanship he had been chosen to lead many groups and committees in all walks of life and was known as the 'master of the meeting'. His death on 3 December 1879 was, incidentally, on the same day and at the same age as the Chairman of the Great Northern Railway, Colonel Duncombe. The Midland Railway's regulation portrait of their chairman had to be painted posthumously.

He was buried at Welford Road cemetery near two other chairmen of the Midland Railway — his father and W.E.Hutchinson who was the father-in-law of Edward's second son, George Henry. In memory of Edward, an annexe was built by subscription in 1884 at the Wyggeston Hospital Boys' School in Applegate and was known as the Ellis Memorial Technical School.[28] It is now part of the Leicester Grammar School. Edward's wife, Emma, lived for a further ten years in The Newarke, the house becoming part of the Leicester College of Art after it was sold to the Corporation in 1893. It was demolished in 1931 to make way for a further section of what is now the Hawthorn building of De Montfort University.

The farmland he owned at Glenfield Frith was sold by the Ellis trustees in 1897.[29] It was purchased by Samuel Faire who erected *Glenfield Frith Hall* on the eastern side of the land which, after his death, became a Dr Barnardos home and the rest of the land a housing development.

John Edward Ellis MP
1841-1910

John Edward Ellis, 1841-1910,
of Nottinghamshire, London and Yorkshire.

Following his childhood at The Newarke in Leicester and attending Quaker schools in Hertford and Kendall, John Edward was given the choice in 1857 of either university education or visiting America with his father. (His father, Edward Shipley Ellis, had financial interests in the Illinois Central Railway [ICR] and wished to visit the company to compare its organisation with that of the Midland Railway as well as wanting to visit relatives.) John decided to travel and was particularly keen to see the railway workshops of the ICR as engineering was an important interest to him. (The President of the ICR made a corresponding visit to the Ellises at Leicester the following year.)

The trip must have been inspirational for John because on his return he joined the Leeds locomotive manufacturers, Kitson & Hewitson, as an apprentice. Having helped build the engines he often went on their testing runs, sometimes working to very tight deadlines that entailed working long hours. On one occasion he was found, back at the factory, sleeping in a boiler that was being riveted above his head! Working with all classes of labour, however, proved useful in later life, although at the time he found the smoky conditions of Leeds distressing (as well as troubling his life-long asthma problem), especially when his grandfather wrote to him about the natural beauty of his country retreat near Woodhouse Eaves.

John's next occupation was at the Hucknall Colliery Company that had been started by four partners, including his father and an uncle, in 1861. At only 20 he was made manager of the mine and was involved with the running of the company (eventually comprising two mines at Hucknall and one at Sherwood that opened in 1902-3) for a further 47 years. Whilst managing the first mine he was continuing his intellectual pursuits and published a paper on Egyptian hieroglyphics.

Like his immediate Ellis forebears John was concerned with the welfare of the local population which included agricultural workers and stocking weavers as well as the miners. He provided Hucknall with reading rooms and a library, and taught at the Adult School — as he had done in his youth at Leicester. He also helped form the local School Board, the first in Nottinghamshire, and was its chairman from 1871 to 1882.

In 1866 he went to Scarborough to recuperate from asthma and on visiting the Quaker's Meeting House there he met Maria Rowntree (of the famous Yorkshire family) whom he married the following year. They lived at various houses in Nottingham — moving to larger premises as their family, started in 1868, grew. John Rowntree was the first-born followed by Arthur Edward, Harold Thornton and twins Marian Emily (eventually Lady Parmoor) and

Edith Maud.[30] In 1878 he invested in a large property in Leicester called *Knighton House*.[31] It is still situated on the corner of London Road and Ratcliffe Road (opposite to *Knighton Hayes*, once owned by his brother, George Henry) but as far as is known he never resided there.

John continued his work outside the collieries at Hucknall. He started a Liberal Association, fought for a piped water supply, formed essay and debating societies, wrote several articles for newspapers and magazines — mainly about political issues — and gave many lectures on social conditions. He developed a real appetite for politics when assisting with the campaign for the 1880 general election and by 1884 was selected as a Liberal candidate for the next general election.

In the meantime he had been made managing director of the Hucknall Colliery Company when his father died in 1879, was appointed chairman of the Joint Stock Bank in 1882 and built his own home, a stone mansion called *Wrea Head*, at Scalby near Scarborough in 1883. This home was in 120 acres, including a 40-acre farm, from where he could carry out his recreations as a naturalist and huntsman.[32]

In 1885 John Edward was elected the first Member of Parliament for the new Rushcliffe division — a seat he held for the next 25 years. For the first 21 of those years he lived at Pont Street, London whenever he was attending the House and later moved to Prince's Gate. He was very active in Parliament making many speeches, especially on Irish Home Rule, in which he took a great deal of interest and visited Ireland on several occasions. He was also a JP for Nottingham borough and county and for the North Riding of Yorkshire.

Particularly distressing periods were when his eldest son died soon after graduating from Cambridge and when his second son died whilst attending the same university two years later. However, his third son, Harold, passed successfully through the university and eventually followed his father as chairman of the Hucknall Colliery Company. Harold married in Canada in 1908 and when John attended the wedding it was the first time he had crossed the Atlantic since visiting America 51 years earlier. (After a terrible crossing on the first trip, presumably by sail, he was thankful that during those years the conditions of the vessels had improved beyond all proportion.)

After an illustrious career in Parliament and being the leading Quaker there, he decided in 1910 to redeem his seat before the next election. He had, during his time in the House, chaired and served on several select and standing committees. He was a member of the Privy Council, Under Secretary of State for India in 1905-06 and in 1909 he joined a mission of peace to Germany where he was assured by the Kaiser that there was no chance of the rumoured war in Europe!

As well as presenting a Temperance Hall in 1894 to the villagers of his adopted home of Scalby, his final act of philanthropy was the gift of a swimming baths to the town of Hucknall in 1909. This was similar to a gift made by his sister-in-law, Rachel Ellis, to the village of Oadby in 1900. Before actually retiring from the House he died on 1 December 1910 at Prince's Gate, still working on political matters that he found so difficult to give up despite failing health.[33,34]

George Henry Ellis
1844-1889

Edward Shipley's second son, George Henry, was working in the family coal and lime business at 16 but then moved to the Whitmore & Ellis Company to concentrate on the worsted spinning side of their business. He was a partner at 22 and remained there for the rest of his short life. He was the last member of the Ellis family connected with the concern.

He married Rachel, the daughter of Quaker, W.E.Hutchinson of Oadby, who was a Leicester chemist and a director (later chairman) of the Midland Railway. George Henry and Rachel lived at *Southfields Villa*, Regent Road (then Regent Street), Leicester before building a house on 8 acres of land at Ratcliffe Road, Stoneygate. Designed by Edward Burgess, the house was called *Knighton Hayes* and was completed in 1880. This very grand building remains today as accommodation for De Montfort University students although a large part of the building, including the stable block on the west side, has been replaced.

George Henry Ellis, 1844-1889, of Knighton Hayes and Sydney Ellis, 1850-1877. (LMARS)

George Henry, a gentleman of unobtrusive disposition, joined the town council in 1881 and was a councillor for three years, serving on several committees until resigning due to ill health. He became a Leicester magistrate in 1884 and was active, like his parents, in the temperance movement becoming treasurer of the Leicester Temperance Society and managing director of the Leicester Coffee & Cocoa House Company. He died, aged only 45, in 1889 without children.

Rachel remained at *Knighton Hayes* almost until her death and will be remembered as a benefactor of Oadby (as was her father) although her first act of benevolence was at Claybrook Magna where she provided land for building the village hall in 1894. At Oadby, in the same year she gave land for the Baptist chapel (although not her religion), provided the recreation ground in Brabazon Road in 1898 which still bears the Ellis family name, and in 1900 gave an indoor swimming baths with library building above (although no longer surviving).[35] She also funded a nursing sister to visit the sick in Oadby until district nurses were provided, and in 1906 contributed £1000 (about a sixth of the total costs)

Rachel, wife of George Henry Ellis. (LMARS)

Knighton Hayes, Ratcliffe Road, built for George Henry and Rachel Ellis in 1880.

MUNICIPAL ELECTION.

TO THE BURGESSES
OF
WEST ST. MARY'S WARD

Ladies and Gentlemen,

In accordance with the wish recently expressed at a meeting of Burgesses, I again offer myself as a candidate for the representation of your Ward on the Council.

Having been connected with West Saint Mary's Ward all my life, it will afford me added pleasure to give attention to any measures which may specially affect your district.

Should you again elect me, it will be my endeavour to uphold that which I believe to be for the advancement and welfare of our town, and to aid in carrying on the important work which is committed to the care of the Council.

I am, yours faithfully,

GEORGE H. ELLIS.

Leicester, October 20, 1882.

Poster for the 1882 local election. Although a radical candidate, canvassing was for the man and not the political party.

for building a new Vaughan College in Leicester. Organisations to which she gave great support were the Bond Street Maternity Hospital, Infant Welfare Movement, Girls' Social Guild and was the local president of the National Union of Women Workers. She died at Scarborough in 1932.

Living not far from *Knighton Hayes* was George Henry's sister, Emily. She died a spinster in 1922 having lived her last 30 years at *Thorncroft* (244) London Road Leicester, which she purchased from travel pioneer, Thomas Cook. It is now the headquarters of the British Red Cross Society.

ALFRED ELLIS
1821-1879

Alfred Ellis, 1821-1879, of Cross Corners and The Brand. (LMARS)

Alfred, the second son of John Ellis, continued to run the farm at Beaumont Leys for three years after his father had left to live at *The Hall* in Belgrave before he too moved to Belgrave following his marriage to Sarah Jane Bowley in 1849. His new house was conveniently situated at the rear of *The Hall*, such that both gardens were treated as one. It was a two-storey Georgian house — later known as *Cross Corners* — and here a family was raised. The children (four boys and three girls that grew to maturity) were fortunate in having at *The Hall* seven of their aunts who were to become regular companions.

Not all was perfect at the house, however, for we know that Alfred was annoyed at two things in particular. Firstly was the odour from the river Soar that flowed nearby causing him — and his father — to write regularly to the authorities in Leicester to complain about the river being used as a sewer. (There were no fish in the river for several miles at that time.) Secondly was the closeness of the *Bull's Head Inn* opposite his home in Thurcaston Road. It had become a run-down, sordid place and so he bought the building and had it demolished in 1860. He gave the land for building a new National School, a fine 'domestic Gothic' structure in granite, completed the following year. This property still stands and is used as offices. (The existing *Bull's Head* public house on the opposite corner was built about ten years later.)

Alfred worked in his father's business, starting on the worsted spinning side but then settled into coal merchandising and the lime business at Barrow-on-Soar. He was also involved with the company slate quarries at Brand Hill, Swithland and Groby. When his father died in 1862 Alfred shared with his two brothers, Edward Shipley and William Henry, the running of John Ellis & Sons and also their new mine at Hucknall Torkard.

Away from business, Alfred was a particularly keen naturalist and at Brand Hill, Woodhouse Eaves, where his father had built a family cottage, he continued his

Cross Corners, Thurcaston Road, Belgrave, once home of Alfred Ellis and other family members.

father's work of planting many different species of trees and shrubs collected from all over Britain (which still flourish today) and laying out the gardens. He even introduced a badger colony (though now a great nuisance) and set up breeding sites for barn owls which, even then, were considered a diminishing species. Alfred corresponded with the eminent naturalists of the time and wrote about the local birds recounting in one book that in his youth he remembered that amazingly there were 626 nests in the rookery around their house at Beaumont Leys and 26 nests in one tree. He also showed a keen interest in the many fossils unearthed at his company's lime workings at Barrow-on-Soar and in the Roman remains which were found there. In fact, a Roman urn became the trademark of the John Ellis Company.

Alfred was auditor to the Leicester Infirmary and a board member from 1858 to 1871. He was on the Belgrave School Board, a county magistrate and in 1874 became a magistrate for

The Brand near Woodhouse Eaves, designed for Alfred Ellis by Alfred Waterhouse and completed in 1875.

Leicester. In that year he also started investing in land. He purchased building plots in Belgrave between Checketts Road and Woodbridge Road — an area where many terraced houses were being built — and by an arrangement with his two brothers, Alfred purchased their share of land at Brand Hill. Most of this was land originally bought by their father and subsequently increased with further purchases by the brothers mostly in 1864.

Here, Alfred decided to build a 'house with offices' and hired the renowned London architect and Quaker, Alfred Waterhouse (creator of many civic buildings including the magnificent Manchester town hall) to carry out the design. Materials specified for its construction included Mountsorrel granite, Yorkshire stone, Barrow lime and oddly, roofing slate from Groby rather than from the family's adjacent Swithland quarries which were still open at that time.[36] The grand house, *The Brand*, was completed in 1875 and its grounds described a few years later as 'unequalled in Leicestershire for their natural and artistic beauty'. The rugged grounds included trout and perch lakes and pike pool converted from the early slate pits.

Unfortunately, Alfred was not able to enjoy the new house for long. He died suddenly at *The Brand* in February 1879 and was buried in Belgrave churchyard (as he and his family had not been Quakers since 1861). In his memory, the chancel screen inside the church is dedicated to him and at Woodhouse Eaves the alter cross in St. Paul's church is dedicated to Alfred and his wife Sarah.

Sarah remained at *The Brand* until 1892 despite part of the land being sold in 1880 and the remaining 51 acres and house sold in 1887. Purchase was by Robert F.Martin of Anstey Pastures (owner of the nearby Mountsorrel Quarries at that time) descendants of whose family still reside at the house.

Only one of Alfred's sons joined the John Ellis company. This was Geoffrey who lived in Prebend Street, Leicester with wife, Agnes, and two daughters — also for a short time at Barrow-on-Soar. He retired to Devon. Two of Alfred's other sons, Walter Bowley and Arthur Guy, had professional occupations in London although Arthur Guy was for a short time involved with the running of the collieries at Hucknall.

William Henry Ellis, 1829-1893,
of Anstey Grange. (LMARS)

WILLIAM HENRY ELLIS
1829-1893

John Ellis's youngest son, William Henry, spent his early years at the Beaumont Leys farm and moved to *The Hall* at Belgrave with his parents and sisters in 1846. He married Caroline Bradley in 1853 moving to a new house in Fosse Road, Newfoundpool, then an elegant suburb of Leicester. They had four boys followed by four girls, the last three girls born when the family had moved to a much larger house called *Anstey Grange* in 1863. This house was situated on Leicester Road, Glenfield at a point between the present County Hall and *The Gynsills* hotel (once home to an Ellis cousin). *Anstey Grange* was a large,Victorian house standing in about 18 acres quite possibly built specially for William Henry.

Trade directories show that William Henry was in the worsted spinning and wool stapling trade (no doubt connected with the Ellis partnership in the John Whitmore Company) for about 20 years, while the 1871 census shows him as a farmer of 38 acres, coal merchant and slate quarry owner. His farming interests were around his home in the Anstey Frith area and the latter two occupations were with John Ellis & Sons. He became controller of this company when the senior partners, brothers Edward Shipley and Alfred, both died in 1879. He was also head of the subsidiary, Ellis, Partridge & Company.

Other business interests included chairman of the Leicester Savings Bank, chairman of the Leicester & Leicestershire Provident Dispensary, chairman of the Leicester Board of the Royal Insurance Company, chairman of the Knighton Junction Brick Company, vice-chairman of the Leicester Waterworks Company, director of Pares's Banking Company and director of the Leicester Coffee & Cocoa House Company — reflecting his temperance views.

Like many of his relatives he was also very involved in public service. He was elected to the Town Council in 1863 and twice was returned for Rothley in the County Council elections. He was a member of the Wyggeston Hospital Trust, a county magistrate from 1882,

Anstey Grange, Leicester Road, Glenfield, seen here in its days as the Grange Hotel.

chairman of the Anstey School Board (following his cousin James), first president of the Leicestershire Adult School Union, a committee member of the Institution & Workshops for the Blind and for a short time Deputy Lieutenant of Leicestershire. He was also president, from 1884 to 1892, of the Harborough Division Liberal Association from which he retired when awarded a year's post as the High Sheriff for Leicestershire.

William Henry died in November 1893 at *Anstey Grange* where his wife, Caroline, continued to live until her death in 1908.

Also there for a short time after William Henry's death was his eldest son, Wilfrid Henry, who had lived for a number of years at *Danesford Villa*, Kirby Road, Leicester. He worked for the John Ellis and Ellis, Partridge companies, was vice president of the Leicester Temperance Society, director of the Leicester Coffee & Cocoa House Company and a County JP. He was at *Anstey Grange* possibly whilst overseeing the erection of two large houses on the 8 acres of land he had purchased in 1900 less than one mile away at Branting Hill near Groby. The larger house, called *Branting Hill*, was used by the Ministry of Defence in the Second World War and eventually became a hotel. It is now known as the *Brant Inn*. Wilfrid Henry lived there approximately between 1901 and 1908, although he retained the house at Kirby Road where he stayed until 1914. The other Groby house was built of stone and demolished when Leicester's Western Bypass was built in the mid 1990s. Wilfrid retired to the south coast in about 1920.

William Henry's second son, Francis Newman, was a director of John Ellis & Sons and of the family's Hucknall Colliery Company. He lived in Nottingham from about 1875 (when he was 20) before moving early in the new century to a grand house at Mansfield Woodhouse called *Debdale Hall*. He lived there until his death in 1934. (The hall is now a nursing home.) Francis Newman was a magistrate for both Mansfield Borough and Nottinghamshire and for the county he was also a councillor, Alderman and Sheriff (1917-18). He succeeded his cousin, John Edward, as chairman of the Hucknall School Board, was a Knight of the Order of St John and a keen mountaineer.[37]

The third son of William Henry was unfortunately 'delicate' and died aged 19, and the youngest son, Owen Alfred, was, like his eldest brother, a director of John Ellis & Sons and the Ellis, Partridge Company. He lived in Leicester until moving in 1898 to a large house called *The Rookery* on Cotes Road, Barrow-on-Soar where he died in 1909. A housing estate now occupies the ground where the house stood appropriately served by a drive called The Rookery.

When sold by the family in 1908, *Anstey Grange* continued as a residence until converted to a boarding house in about 1938. It subsequently became the *Grange Hotel*, but was demolished when the A50 was widened near to the County Hall in the early 1970s.

BELGRAVE HALL and
JOHN ELLIS'S SEVEN DAUGHTERS

Belgrave is only two miles north of Leicester and *The Hall*, John Ellis's second home, still stands in Church Road (once The Gravel) off Thurcaston Road. It is in a secluded part of the old village, away from the mainly residential developments of the later nineteenth and early twentieth centuries to the south and east of the village.

After much refurbishment to house and garden, John and Priscilla Ellis, with their seven daughters (though not Lucy initially) and youngest son moved into *The Hall* in 1846. Surprisingly the house was not much larger than the one they left at Beaumont Leys, but grand living was not part of the Quaker tradition. The three-storey building is in a plain Queen Anne style of brick and was built between 1709 and 1713 for Edmund Cradock. The main occupants were the Vann family who owned the property from 1767 to 1844 and who also built *Belgrave House* on part of the paddock on the opposite side of Church Road. The paddock (now a park) stretched down to the river Soar and once included a summerhouse and boathouse with room above. At the rear of The Hall, John Ellis, a keen horticulturalist, had the formal and informal walled gardens immaculately maintained, the gardens containing traditional and exotic plants and shrubs, fernery, fruit trees (including mulberries which still produce a good crop) and a Dutch garden.

When they moved into *The Hall*, the age of the seven daughters, Lucy, Eliza, Jane, Isabella, Margaret, Charlotte and Ellen Maria, ranged from 7 to 24, but despite the variance

The front elevation of Belgrave Hall, a museum since 1937.

they were all very well educated at home by one tutor, Lydia Rous, who later became head mistress of the Mount School at York.[38,39] Although daughters of a farmer and therefore considered middle class and not gentry, they were probably the best educated and emancipated women in the district. By quoting from *'Records of Nineteenth Century Leicester'* we can get an idea of their persona: '. . . they were in touch with all the best literature and the leading movements of the nineteenth century . . . they exhibited a dignity, a distinction and a charm that set them, in a busy provincial town, in a class apart. In no way inhuman, if somewhat Wordsworthian, they did not always see eye-to-eye, and could on occasion firmly speak the truth in love, one to another. But they radiated affection to a large and ever widening family circle, and maintained an unbroken front of benevolence toward the outer world.'

They also took a keen interest in politics, being active Liberals and followers of the Women's Suffrage movement (though never militant). They were dedicated to their Quaker beliefs and were active members of several charities, organising and trying to solve the problems of the poor. This is shown in 1874 when they started the Town Mission to teach reading, writing and religion to adults. Meetings were first held in the laundry of *The Hall*, but in 1877 moved to a Quaker property in Bath Street where a rebuilt hall, the Belgrave Adult School, remains today.[40] It was one of the first establishments for adult education outside a major town. Before this the sisters had started a school for infants in the village around 1871.

Book meetings were held regularly at *The Hall* where members of the Society of Friends would meet to exchange books and read their own essays. Writing was a particular talent of the sisters especially Eliza, Margaret and Charlotte. Eliza, although sickly, was very academic. For instance, she read Plato, carried out experiments, avidly collected fossils and wrote huge amounts of letters about her various interests to friends and relatives — many to her former tutor, Lydia Rous. After she died at the comparatively young age of 54, Margaret collected many of her letters and from them compiled a book of great literary merit for private circulation entitled 'Letters and Memorials of Eliza Ellis'. Margaret also wrote many articles for magazines.

Charlotte was the genealogist of the family and wrote 'Sketches of one Branch of the Ellis Family' an excellent early history of their own and related families. Jointly with her cousin, Hannah Ellis, she was secretary of the Leicester Charity Organisation Society from when it was founded in 1876, and in 1888 was one of the first women on the Board of Guardians.[41] This board administered poor relief on behalf of the borough and she came across very grim and distressing situations in this position, but carried on the work for nine years. It was whilst on this committee that she and thousands of others — especially in Leicestershire — rigorously campaigned against compulsory smallpox vaccination.[42] Because of her leading role in the protest, prosecution was threatened and she only narrowly missed a jail sentence when family and friends persuaded her to stand down.

Charlotte and Ellen Ellis. Their relatively plain dresses were typically Quaker in style. (LMARS)

Jane organised mothers' meetings at Belgrave to try helping with their problems and she, along with Charlotte and Margaret, was on the local committee of the Women's Liberal Association. Isabella was a tall, cheerful person despite enduring severe back problems most of her life and confined to an invalid chair for long periods. Her great interest was ornithology and her knowledge was quite extensive.

In fact, all the sisters enjoyed their natural surroundings — probably stemming from their country upbringing at Beaumont Leys where they often returned on nostalgic walks. Frequent trips were also made to the family cottage at Brand Hill, near Woodhouse Eaves, where they sometimes stayed, two or three at a time, for several days studying, writing, sketching, painting and so on (Jane was the true artist). They also travelled much further afield, visiting at some stage nearly all areas of Britain and even touring as far as Germany and Switzerland. One family holiday in 1866 lasted for two months when they stayed on the shores of Loch Goil in Scotland and on occasions some of the sisters travelled to Ireland to stay with their uncle James.

When staying at Belgrave, Sunday mornings were spent attending the Quaker meeting hall in Leicester (once at Soar Lane, but from 1877 to 1955 in Prebend Street). They would ride there in the smart family phaeton driven by a liveried coachman and as they were so well known, their drive through the town became a regular spectacle for passers-by. When travelling along Belgrave Road they would have witnessed many changes over the years — like the urban sprawl of houses and factories between village and town, the erection of the Great Northern railway station and the disappearance of the adjacent stream that would have been forded by their carriage.

Only two of the sisters married — the eldest and youngest — both in middle age. In 1876 Lucy married a widower, Joseph Stickney Sewell who had been married to a cousin of Lucy's in Yorkshire and was the editor of a monthly journal. They lived at the neighbouring house, *Cross Corners* (which brother Alfred had recently vacated) and spent some time on charity work in Madagascar.

Ellen Maria married Alfred Priestman in 1887 and lived in Yorkshire. Ellen had been the vice-chairman of the governors of the Wyggeston Hospital Girls' School in Humberstone Gate from when it opened in 1878.

The last of the sisters died in 1923. This was Margaret and at her Easter Monday funeral Theodore Ellis, son of their cousin James, gave an address, a few lines of which sums up their lives: 'They were public-spirited citizens, beloved and looked up to in Belgrave and Leicester. Their home was one of culture and refinement. Their outlook on the world was wide.' Four of the sisters were buried in Belgrave cemetery.

In 1923 *Belgrave Hall*, as it was then known, was sold to Thomas Morley, a Leicester hosier (who had, coincidently, been living at another former Ellis property, *The Cedars* in Glenfield Frith) and in 1936 it was purchased by Leicester Corporation for use as a museum and botanical garden. It was opened to the public the following year and has been subsequently run by Leicestershire County Council and now the City Council. It attracted the world media in December 1998 when, following sightings in earlier years, there was conjectural camera evidence of a female ghost in the rear garden. However, the picture was not sufficiently clear to see if it were one of the seven sisters.

JOHN ELLIS & SONS LTD

John Ellis's venture into business started with the trading of produce from his Beaumont Leys farm, and by 1827 he was partnering his brother, Joseph, selling their homegrown corn and Joseph's malt at premises in Leicester. From 1832, following the major part he played in the instigation of the Leicester & Swannington Railway, John then concentrated on selling coal brought from the Leicestershire coalfields to the canal-side at West Bridge. From here his company was to trade for the next 132 years. The railway also brought lime to the site from Breedon, which he sold along with the same commodity transported by canal from the county's other major lime-field at Barrow-on-Soar.

Following the opening of the Midland Counties Railway in 1840 coal and lime was also sold from the wharves at Leicester and Syston and a further depot opened soon after at Soar Lane, only about a quarter-of-a-mile north of West Bridge.

The lime business did particularly well and in the early 1840s the company (by then John Ellis & Sons) was renting land at Barrow-on-Soar to extract and burn limestone in their own kilns. Barrow lime had been used for centuries and produced a strong mortar, even setting under water (reputedly used for building dams in Holland, but certainly for seaside pier foundations and extensively on the London underground) and excellent for agricultural purposes and sewage treatment. Demand was increasing, especially for the rapid growth of factory and house building in the second half of the nineteenth century, and the lime was shipped out to all parts of the country by the conveniently adjacent railway and canal systems. By 1886 there were more than 30 kilns on the site which covered over 80 acres and was situated a mile south of Barrow, mostly between the Sileby road and railway line, although some lime-fields were east of the line. The extraction sites (delphs) and the kilns were linked by a 3ft-gauge railway that was replaced by one of standard gauge track in 1920.[43]

Another commodity in which the company traded was Swithland slate, the amount of which increased when, in 1851, John and Joseph Ellis bought 41 acres of land at Brand Hill, Woodhouse Eaves that included some old slate workings.[44] These were opened up mainly to manufacture roofing slates, although a small proportion was used for a variety of products such as walling, headstones and thralls. It was a strange time to open up the quarries as roofing slate was being increasingly shipped from North Wales and, although less durable, was a far more manageable and cost-effective material.

3ft gauge 'Tynemouth' and standard gauge 'Charnwood', both Hunslet engines which were used at the Barrow-on-Soar lime works. ('Charnwood', G. Alliez)

However, markets for the home product must have been good; although the small quarries at Brand Hill were closed in the 1860s, at the same time, larger ones were rented and reopened by the company at Swithland (the ancient 'great pit' in Swithland Woods) and two at Groby.[45] Maybe winning two large contracts helped: firstly was the provision of thousands of slate walling blocks and piles for building Cropston reservoir in 1866-70 (perhaps a guaranteed order as the company chairman, Edward Shipley Ellis, was at the time also chairman of the Leicester Waterworks Company for which the reservoir was being built) and secondly, the supply of Groby slates for roofing and paving at the Midland Railway's new hotel at St Pancras station, which opened in 1873. (Maybe another guaranteed order, as Edward was also chairman of the Midland Railway.)

Along with the supply of roofing slate, a roofing service was set up and this led to the formation of a subsidiary firm — Ellis, Partridge & Company — which was to work solely in slate from Wales and North-West England when the supply of roofing materials from Swithland and Groby finished effectively in 1887.

With the opening of the Leicester & Hitchin Railway in 1857, John Ellis & Sons had new outlets for coal and lime when wharves were opened at Wigston Magna, Great Glen and Kibworth stations. Later, near this line, in about 1870, another lime-burning operation was being run by the company at Kilby Bridge, one mile south of Wigston, but on a much smaller scale than Barrow. This business was probably taken over from a William Bray who was the sole lime-burner there before that time. The works covered about 25 acres, mostly between the railway and canal on the east side of the A50 and a special rail siding was put in for the despatch of lime and receipt of the large amounts of coal required in the burning process (almost a quarter of a ton per ton of lime produced). The transport was shared with the adjacent canal, and coal was also traded from Kilby Bridge.

The depot at Leicester on the former Midland Counties line, which was approached from Southampton Street during the 1850s and 60s, was moved to the Humberstone Road coal wharf where it remained for over 100 years. Also, a head office was set up in about 1870 at 8 Market Street, Leicester, before moving to larger premises at 1 St Martins in 1894, the year the firm was converted into a limited company. Depots were opened for just a few years at Broughton Astley and Belgrave Road canal wharf in the 1880s and for only one year at the Great Central Railway's new wharf at Western Boulevard in 1899. However, Broughton

---

GROBY AND SWITHLAND SLATE QUARRIES.

JOHN ELLIS & SONS,

PROPRIETORS,

LEICESTER.

JOHN ELLIS & SONS since entering on the above Works have, by the erection of suitable Machinery, put themselves in a position to supply promptly the various articles for which this durable and excellent material is used, comprising :—

Roofing Slates, suitable for all purposes, and especially for Gothic Buildings.

Gravestones, plain or engraved, Chimney-pieces, Door Steps, Window and Door Sills.

Flagging, Sawn and dressed, Kerbstones, Garden Edging.

Cisterns, Baths, Sinks, Gate Posts, Pier Caps, Cheese Presses, Milk Slates and Salting Troughs, Coping, Wall and Road Stones, &c.

A good supply of self-faced SLABS for covering wells, tanks, and flat arches to 10 feet span. Also, rough Slabs, cheap and valuable for footings and foundations.

Prices and other particulars can be obtained from MR. W. H. ELLIS, 47 King Street, Leicester ; or MR. S. WILLSON, Groby ; and orders received at the West Bridge Wharf, where a stock is kept.

An advertisement from the 1868 edition of 'Spencer's Leicester Almanack' for John Ellis slate products.

Astley, and then depots at Thurnby and Glen Parva (Blaby canal wharf), were sold to Joseph Ellis & Sons, and Great Glen and Kibworth to Ellis & Everard in 1899/1900.

But the major company activity was at Barrow-on-Soar where, as well as producing lime, firstly plaster and then cement, using the Portland process, was manufactured from about 1888. (Cement technology was improving rapidly at this time and it was found that good silica shale that is necessary to produce strong cement when burnt with the lime could be shipped from the Kilby Bridge area.) This led to the development of the core business of John Ellis & Sons — the manufacture of concrete products which started in the 1890s. The main aggregate used in making the concrete was granite chippings which was readily available from the nearby

JNO. ELLIS & SONS,
COAL, LIME, & SLATE
MERCHANTS.

JNO. ELLIS & SONS are prepared to execute Orders for the Celebrated

Netherseal, Old Swanwick,
REAL KILBURNE, COTMANHAY,
OR ANY OTHER DESCRIPTION OF COAL.

ORDERS SENT TO THEIR OFFICES AT

WEST BRIDGE, SOAR LANE,
AND
HUMBERSTONE ROAD WHARVES,

OR TO THEIR CENTRAL OFFICE,—

8, MARKET STREET, LEICESTER,
WILL RECEIVE PROMPT ATTENTION.

Truck Loads of Crich Lime and any description of Coal supplied at Country Stations at Colliery Weights, and at the lowest possible prices.

Agents for Messrs. JOSEPH ELLIS & SONS'

ARTIFICIAL MANURES, &c.

PROPRIETORS OF THE

GROBY & SWITHLAND SLATE QUARRIES.

ORDERS FOR ABOVE, ALSO, FOR

BARROW AND KILBY BRIDGE LIME
RECEIVED AT
8, MARKET STREET, LEICESTER.
22

An 1878 advertisement for the various commodities of John Ellis & Sons.

Just east of Kilby Bridge on the Grand Union Canal is Ellis's Bridge which gave access to the lime works.

Mountsorrel quarries. In fact, huge amounts of granite had been shipped by rail from Mountsorrel past the lime works to the main line railhead at Barrow since 1860.

Initially, paving slabs, kerbs and sewer tubes were the main products and there followed reinforced structural components like roof beams, stairways and flooring. Other products included reservoirs, water towers, fence and gateposts, telegraph and railway signal columns and swimming baths. Marble terrazzo and mosaic floors and artificial stone resembling traditional Weldon, Portland and Ketton stone, for use on building facings, was also supplied. Sewer tubes and artificial stone were the main products sold through London offices when they first opened in 1903 and maintained there for most years until the 1960s.

By 1912 the Leicester office had moved to 16

A company letter heading from 1910.

Pocklingtons Walk, and at that time there were two grandsons of John Ellis on the board of directors, Wilfrid Henry Ellis of Leicester and Francis Newman Ellis of *Debdale Hall*, Mansfield Woodhouse — the last Ellises working for the company. The managing director was William C.Sharman, an in-law of a third grandson, Owen Alfred Ellis.

It was William Sharman who planned the merger of John Ellis & Sons with the Mountsorrel Granite Company which took effect in January 1920. Three directors from the Ellis company were on the new board: F.N.Ellis, W.C.Sharman, and J.E.Hodding (husband of John Ellis's grand-daughter, Isabel Mary) but the two companies were still run independently.

The directors must have been confident in the company's prospects as in the following year 50 acres of land was purchased at Barrow on either side of the railway line to which was added 18 acres six years later. From 1924 there was also a third member of the group when the Enderby & Stoney Stanton Granite Company was acquired.

To increase the excavation of shale at Kilby Bridge — and also limestone as the quarrying of lime had ceased at Barrow in the early 1920s — a new drag-line was purchased in 1925. However, it was only in use for a few years as it was found that the necessary minerals for producing cement could be purchased more cheaply from Wirksworth in Derbyshire. The Kilby Bridge site was consequently closed in 1931. The coal trade there had already stopped in 1928 and from 1931 a few of the John Ellis coal depots elsewhere were run as an independent concern. This was set up in conjunction with Joseph Ellis & Sons Ltd under the name of John & Joseph Ellis Ltd based at the Pocklingtons Walk office.[46] The only depots retained were at Humberstone Road, West Bridge and Syston. At Kilby Bridge, the Ellis land, including a farm and cottages, was sold in 1948.

The John Ellis company henceforth

An example of how manufactured stone was used by the John Ellis company at the Westleigh cinema, Fosse Road South, Leicester in 1926. The cinema's internal marble staircase was also supplied.

An advertising postcard from the 1930s showing 11 lorries (mostly belonging to Edlins and Kinders transport) loaded with a consignment of concrete sewer tubes. They are outside John Ellis & Sons' main office at Barrow-on-Soar.

concentrated on the expanding concrete market. Land had been purchased in 1928 at Potters Marston, conveniently by the railway just north of the Stoney Stanton quarries, and certain concrete items were produced there using the readily available granite. In 1930, the head office for the group was set up in the new *Welford House*, Welford Place, Leicester, and the following year an additional office block was built on the production site at Sileby Road, Barrow.

For years, experiments to improve the spinning process in concrete tube manufacture had been carried out at Barrow, but a superior method, the Hume process from Australia, was used when tube production was transferred to Potters Marston (after purchasing more land) in 1937. However, only three years later the main product at the branch was not tubes but concrete air-raid shelters. These were so urgently required at the beginning of the War that production continued day and night for several months. New concrete products at Barrow

A Scene from the 1950s; an Atkinson lorry ready to deliver 'Ellispun' concrete pipes.

were pit props, fences for the War Department and railway sleepers. 'Tarren' compressed boards were also made from limestone and sawdust and used for army huts and in the temporary repair of bombed houses. For the same purpose breeze blocks were also made at Potters Marston, the company at that time, and until 1946, working under the Government's Essential Works Order. After the War up to 60 German prisoners-of-war were employed by the firm.

Two products for which the company was well known before and after hostilities were Emalux, a glazed cement wall finish, and Ellicem, a special type of cement paint. In 1947 the manufacture of their own cement was given up in preference to that produced at Ketton and in that year the head office was moved from Welford Place to 21 New Walk (with extra office space bought at 32 and 6 Princess Road in 1953 and 1958 respectively).

The early 1950s were profitable with contracts like 500 'Wates' prefabricated houses and 14,000 tons of concrete blocks for Pitford reservoir, and in 1952 a further 64 acres of land was purchased in Barrow. In 1955, 50,000 tons of concrete products were despatched from Barrow and 35,000 tons from Potters Marston.

Perhaps because of their success the group was acquired by Redland Holdings Ltd in 1960, who initially maintained the names of the individual companies within the group. By 1973, however, the name 'John Ellis & Sons' ceased to exist and the New Walk office closed, although concrete products — mainly specialist paving, kerbs and building blocks — continued to be produced at Barrow and tubes at Potters Marston. This latter site was closed in 1980 (now a large bottled-gas depot) and Redlands were taken over by Lafarge Aggregates Ltd in 1997.

ELLIS, PARTRIDGE & COMPANY (LEICESTER) LTD

One commodity in which the John Ellis company had traded since 1836 was roofing slates, later obtained from their own Leicestershire quarries, and then mainly from North Wales. By 1877 a subsidiary had been started, Ellis, Wormell & Company, to concentrate on the selling and installation of the slates, the company operating from the John Ellis head office at 8 Market Street and from the house of the manager, Arthur B Partridge, at 8 Brunswick Street, Leicester. The partners in the company were William Henry Ellis, his sons, Wilfrid Henry and Owen Alfred and also Robert Wormell, a member of a family that had run slating businesses in Leicester since before the 1830s and even now continue an operation in Warwickshire.

By 1881 Wormell was no longer working for the company and Arthur Partridge became a new partner in the firm which was renamed Ellis, Partridge & Company, trading from 10 Market Street and the LNW Railway wharf at Humberstone Road (from where they traded for the following 86 years) as well as Brunswick Street. By that date they were also supplying a large range of building materials and making their own bricks and tiles. Where these were made initially is not known, but by 1891 they had a factory at Woodville, Derbyshire complete with their own railway sidings. Some of their materials were probably also made by the Knighton Junction Brick Company Ltd as William Henry Ellis was also a director of that

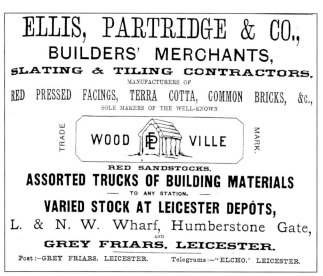

ELLIS, PARTRIDGE & CO.,
BUILDERS' MERCHANTS,
SLATING & TILING CONTRACTORS.
MANUFACTURERS OF
RED PRESSED FACINGS, TERRA COTTA, COMMON BRICKS, &c.,
SOLE MAKERS OF THE WELL-KNOWN

TRADE   WOOD [EP] VILLE   MARK.

RED SANDSTOCKS.

ASSORTED TRUCKS OF BUILDING MATERIALS
— TO ANY STATION. —
VARIED STOCK AT LEICESTER DEPÔTS,
L. & N. W. Wharf, Humberstone Gate,
AND
GREY FRIARS, LEICESTER.

Post:—GREY FRIARS, LEICESTER.   Telegrams:—"ELCHO," LEICESTER.

*Ellis, Partridge were merchants, contractors and manufacturers of
building materials as this advertisement of 1899 shows.*

concern, and by 1891 they shared their head offices at *Conway Buildings*, Greyfriars, Leicester — a grand three-storey building of 1878, which still exists.

Before the turn of the century Ellis, Partridge & Company also traded in Bristol, but only for a few years, unlike their outlets in London that were open for their roofing contracting business from the 1880s to the mid 1950s.

On becoming a limited company in about 1931, the business name was changed to Ellis, Partridge & Company (Leicester) Ltd, and in the early 1940s yet another change occurred. This was when James Kibert, who had been with the company for about 20 years, was made a partner and the company became Ellis, Partridge, Kibert & Company Ltd with a new head office at 136 New Walk. Less than five years later it was Ellis, Partridge & Company (Leicester) Ltd again, a name retained until local business ceased in 1967 when the main office was briefly at 106 London Road.

SECTION 2
JOSEPH ELLIS - HIS DESCENDANTS AND COMPANIES

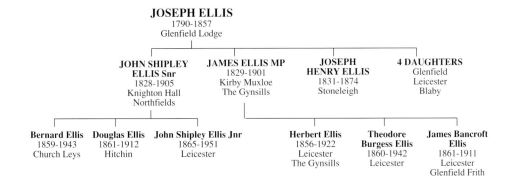

JOSEPH ELLIS
1790-1857
Glenfield Lodge

JOHN SHIPLEY ELLIS Snr 1828-1905 Knighton Hall Northfields	**JAMES ELLIS MP** 1829-1901 Kirby Muxloe The Gynsills	**JOSEPH HENRY ELLIS** 1831-1874 Stoneleigh	**4 DAUGHTERS** Glenfield Leicester Blaby

Bernard Ellis 1859-1943 Church Leys	**Douglas Ellis** 1861-1912 Hitchin	**John Shipley Ellis Jnr** 1865-1951 Leicester	**Herbert Ellis** 1856-1922 Leicester The Gynsills	**Theodore Burgess Ellis** 1860-1942 Leicester	**James Bancroft Ellis** 1861-1911 Leicester Glenfield Frith

JOSEPH ELLIS
1790-1857

Joseph was running the family farm at *Sharman's Lodge* when his father died in 1810. He probably continued to farm there until 1816, when the estate from which the farm was leased was sold and the buildings extended by the new owner. Between then and 1824, the year we know he was at his next farm, Joseph had speculated and lost a large amount of money. He had invested in a Derbyshire lead-smelting concern whose product had been 'salted' to show a high silver content and this swindle left him near penniless. (His investment may have been the comparatively large amount of £1,000 his father had bequeathed to each of his children.)

However, his family rallied to his cause and by 1824, after a brief spell living in Glenfield village, he was occupying a farm called *Glenfield Lodge* with his new wife, Hannah Shipley of Uttoxeter (she was the sister of his brother

Joseph Ellis, 1790-1857, of Glenfield Lodge.

39

John's first wife, Martha). *Glenfield Lodge* is shown on contemporary maps to be on the Kirby Muxloe side of Glenfield between Stamford Street and *Kirby Frith Hall* and most probably a former name of *Manor Farm*. This was a large, seventeenth-century house that survived until a housing development covered the site in the 1980s. It appears from directories that when the property was vacated by the Ellises around 1863, it was occupied by a family called Tebbs who were probably responsible for the change in name.

In the year Joseph was married, William, the first of eight children was born, followed by Mary, John Shipley, James, Joseph Henry, Hannah, Sarah Anne and lastly Sophia in 1838.

By 1827 Joseph was in business partnering his elder brother, John, as a corn dealer and maltster in Leicester, and following his involvement in the instigation of the Leicester & Swannington Railway (of which he was a director from 1831 to 1846) another partnership was entered in 1832. This was with a gentleman called Sims with whom he sold coal brought down the new line to the station at Glenfield. However, because of a disagreement, this partnership did not last, but it was the forerunner of a business primarily in selling coal that was to run for a very long time. He was next selling coal on the Midland Counties Railway,

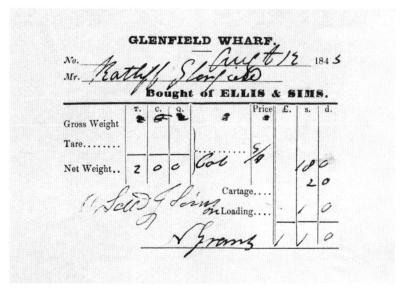

For a few years Joseph Ellis was in partnership with J. Sims at Glenfield station on the Leicester & Swannington line. This is a sales receipt from 1845.

opened in 1840, which proved to be the start of his own company, eventually to become Joseph Ellis & Sons Ltd.

His dealing in corn and brewing malt continued, not with John, but in partnership with his youngest brother, Robert, who had returned to the county from Yorkshire. This shared business was run from Highcross Street, Leicester with Joseph making the malt from his own barley at Glenfield. He probably carried out the process at the 'Meeting House' in Glenfield Square as he was renting the property from the 'Society of Quakers' at the time and the building had long been used for the malting process. He also made the malt for the local farmers who provided their own barley. Joseph was involved with this business almost until his death.

Like John, he entered local politics, but only briefly, being elected once as a Leicester councillor in 1839.

With the money he was making from corn, malt and coal, Joseph started to buy farmland in the Glenfield area. In doing this he obviously had knowledge of land values which led to another phase in his life. Briefly, in 1843, he was assessing compensation for landowners on the newly-opened Midland Counties Railway (as his eldest brother had done) and then from 1845 he was employed by the Midland Railway to value and negotiate for land in preparation for building their Syston and Peterborough branch. No doubt, the fact that John Ellis was chairing the Construction Committee of the line at the time had some bearing on Joseph's appointment. Joseph worked occasionally on the line until 1849.

Also employed in a similar role on the line was a farmer from Groby, Breedon Everard. Although 24 years his junior, he must have collaborated well with Joseph as they decided to form a partnership to sell coal and other commodities that could be brought cheaply to the stations on the new railway. Their first depot was opened at Stamford in 1848 and depots followed at most of the other stations on the line. Thus, the well-known company of Ellis & Everard was founded and many depots were subsequently opened on other lines.

In the census of 1851 Joseph's occupation was entered as 'land agent and valuer, coal merchant and farmer of 450 acres' (much of the land he farmed was in Glenfield and partly rented from bank owner, Thomas Pares, and partly from John Sydney Crossley, a renowned railway engineer from Barrow-on-Soar). In his role as land agent a tale is told of an incident that occurred when Joseph was riding home having collected rent in Nuneaton. He was confronted by a highwayman with pistol in hand, and so spurred his horse and jumped at the man, knocking him out of his saddle before riding on. About a year later Joseph saw the same man at Market Bosworth standing trial for highway robbery.[47]

Another commodity in which Messrs Ellis and Everard saw potential was granite, as this was being used increasingly for road metalling at that time. They purchased a quarry in Markfield in 1852 and four years later planned the opening of a further quarry at Bardon Hill. Surprisingly, Joseph continued to run his own coal business independently of 'Ellis & Everard', but it did enable Joseph's two younger sons, James and Joseph Henry to enter into the partnership of both companies when they were ready to start their careers in the early 1850s. Of the two elder sons, William had died when only 15 and John Shipley continued to work on the family farm at *Glenfield Lodge*. He had to oversee the farm when his father was taken ill and moved with his four daughters to *Glenfield House* in the centre of the village in 1856. Here, Joseph died on 21 March 1857 aged 66.

During his life in Glenfield Joseph had been a respected gentleman and an integral part of the village community. Despite being a staunch Quaker he was an advocate of religious freedom and was even treasurer to the local Wesleyan Sunday school. Due to the time of his death, one building he was unable to see complete was the new corn exchange in Leicester for which he was a member of the construction committee.[48] It opened on 1 August 1857 with three of its permanent stalls taken by Ellis companies. Joseph was buried in Welford Road cemetery, the first of many family members.

The first family home at *Sharman's Lodge*[49] was demolished when a huge mansion, *Frith House*, was completed on the estate in 1873. This imposing stone building, once a hospital for servicemen and then a home for the mentally ill, remains as an administrative unit of the Fosse Health Trust near to Glenfield Hospital.

JOHN SHIPLEY ELLIS (SENIOR)
1828-1905

Glenfield Lodge was home to Joseph's eldest son, John Shipley, for his first 35 years, but in 1863 he left the 360 acres he was then farming for completely different surroundings at *Melbourne House*, 26 Princess Street (later Princess Road) in Leicester. He moved to work in the partnership of his late father's Leicester-based business, Joseph Ellis & Sons and later at Ellis & Everard, companies for which he worked the rest of his life. Moving with him was Silena, his wife since 1856, and his first four children. Five other children were born in the new house (two dying in infancy) before he moved in about 1879 to a much grander home, the seventeenth century *Knighton Hall*. This stands in Church Lane and was the family home for about 13 years. At one time it was from the hall's stables that horses were sent to West Bridge to carry out deliveries for the Ellis companies.[50]

John Shipley's next house was the almost equally large *Northfields* in Gipsy Lane, Leicester where he moved in 1892.

John Shipley Ellis Snr, 1828-1905, with wife Silena. (LMARS)

The house was then standing in open countryside, but the area eventually became part of Leicester's urbanisation and as such *Northfields*, after use as a training centre for the Ministry of Labour in the 1930s and 40s, was converted to a junior school, Northfield House, from about 1950.

Knighton Hall, Church Lane, home of John Shipley Ellis snr and now the residence of the Vice Chancellor of the University of Leicester.

John Shipley moved for the last time in 1902 from *Northfields* to *Cross Corners*, Belgrave (once the home of his cousin Alfred) where he died in 1905 whilst still chairman, as he had been since 1899, of Joseph Ellis & Sons and

Ellis & Everard. Silena also died there in 1913 and it was home to two of their daughters, Marian and Agnes. *Cross Corners* became a home for mentally-deficient boys in the late 1920s. It then reverted to use as a private residence until 1959 when it became an annex of the Belgrave Hall museum. It is a listed Grade II building.

All of John Shipley's four sons — Bernard, Douglas, John Shipley (junior) and Somers How, held senior positions in both of the Ellis companies he controlled — although Somers How became a consulting civil engineer, spending some time in China, and was a director for only one year. Subsequent generations were the mainstay of the companies for many years.

Bernard Ellis, 1859-1943, of Church Leys.

Bernard Ellis
1859-1943

Following his education in York and two years working in Bristol, where he learned accountancy, Bernard joined the two family businesses in 1878 and from then lived most of his life in Leicester. After leaving his parent's home at *Knighton Hall* in about 1892 his own Leicester homes were at *Moat House* in East Park Road, Kirby Road and Avenue Road, Stoneygate.

When living at *Moat House* he married Isabel Clare Evans whose grandfather was the renowned Joseph Dare, a minister who campaigned with great influence during the third quarter of the 1800s for decent housing, education, pure water and sanitation for Leicester's impoverished. Isabel, a tireless social worker, was president of the Leicester Health Society, a member of the new Leicester School Board and joint initiator of both the Bond

Street Maternity Hospital and Leicester University College. She also wrote books of local interest including the very useful *'Records of Nineteenth Century Leicester'*, a book of historical importance which looks into the lives of many families including the Ellises.

Bernard was a Leicester magistrate, secretary of the local NSPCC, the 1916-17 president of the Leicestershire Literary & Philosophical Society and chairman of the governors of

Church Leys at Rearsby, now a nunnery.
(LMARS)

Wyggeston Hospital from 1922 to 1941. A stone tablet inside the hospital in his honour is inscribed: 'He is gratefully remembered for his personal interest in the welfare of the inmates of the hospital and for his wise administration of the estates of the charity'. He was a senior partner in Joseph Ellis & Sons and Ellis & Everard from 1886, chairman of the former from 1906 and the latter from1922.

They had a daughter and three sons — all of whom had Bernard as a middle name including daughter, Christine. Only the eldest son Colin Dare and Christine (just briefly) joined the two Ellis companies. For their final years the family moved in 1920 to a large, Victorian, gabled house, once a hunting box (with stables for 12 horses) called *Church Leys*, in Rearsby. It had previously been the home of the Countess of Cowley. Whilst there, Isabel died in 1936 and Bernard in 1943. Soon after, the house became a nunnery and retreat — 'The Novitiate of the Sisters of St Joseph of Peace' — as it remains today.

Christine, the eldest child, devoted most of her life to community work. She worked for the Friends' Relief Service in Serbia and Holland during and just after the First World War, and did similar work in Bulgaria in the 1920s. Her relief work was continued during the Second World War when she was also a governor of Ackworth School and a member of the Friends' Education Council.

Colin Dare Bernard Ellis, 1895-1969.

The eldest son, Colin Dare Bernard Ellis, became a prominent member of the Ellis family, not so much in a public role as other leading members, but mainly for his writing and as a historian.[51] His interest in these topics was most probably inherited from his mother, but his initial education followed that of his father at Bootham School. From here, Colin went to King's College, Cambridge before joining the colours in the First World War in which, as a lieutenant in the Leicestershire Royal Horse Artillery, he was awarded the Military Cross for conspicuous gallantry and devotion to duty under heavy shell fire. He was acting as a forward observing officer sending back valuable information and was severely wounded.

After the War, he returned to *Church Leys* and soon became secretary and director of Ellis & Everard and director of Joseph Ellis & Sons. In 1922 he married Ethel Vavasour Clarke, living in Woodgate, Rothley where two daughters were born. *Stafford Lodge*, Quorndon was his next home from 1926, and whilst there his first books were published. Two were of poetry entitled *'The Dispassionate Pilgrim'* and *'Mournful Numbers'* (from which two extracts are shown in appendix III) and these were followed by *'Historical Guide to the City of Leicester'*, written with S.H.Skillington. Around this time he started a keen interest in riding with the Quorn hunt.

In 1935 he moved to a larger house, *Benscliffe House*, Ulverscroft which was his home for about 24 years. At this time he was president of the Leicestershire Literary & Philosophical Society of which he was also long-time secretary. Through this society he was selected chairman of a committee that controlled the excavations of the Roman, Jewry Wall site in the years before the Second World War. He showed 'inspiring enthusiasm' in this role and was elected a Fellow of the Society of Antiquaries in 1940 for his services to archaeology. During the Second World War he was appointed director of Home Grown Cereals in the Ministry of Food, a post that took him to Colwyn Bay for four years.

An important literary work was his *'History in Leicester'*, first published in 1948. There were further editions in 1969 and 1976 and the book has become a standard work on the city's history. Prior to its writing he had completed two centenary histories: of Joseph Ellis & Sons Ltd in 1939 and of Ellis & Everard Ltd in 1948, both of which were privately published. His other main publication was *'Leicestershire and the Quorn Hunt'* of 1951. This was a comprehensive study, considered to be one of the most scholarly histories of a hunt ever written.

Over many years he compiled a vast list of monumental inscriptions in the churches and chapels of the county and their graveyards, a record of great benefit to historians. He was also a prolific writer of small historical articles, many published in the Leicestershire & Rutland Magazine in the 1940s and in the transactions of the Leicestershire Archaeological & Historical Society. He was president of this society from 1961 to 1966 and president emeritus until his death.

In 1955 he was awarded the CBE for his services during the Second World War and to the local community in a number of capacities mainly connected with education and the arts. For more than 20 years he was a co-opted member of the Leicester Museums & Library Committee (particularly advising on the purchase of paintings), was vice-chairman of the Governors of Wyggeston Hospital and a trustee of the Leicester General Charities and of Bradgate Park. He was also a member of the Council of the University College and president of the National Association of Corn & Agricultural Merchants.

Already a director of the Leicester Temperance Building Society, he was made chairman of Joseph Ellis & Sons in 1944 and chairman of Ellis & Everard from 1952 until 1965. By this time he had returned to live at Rothley, before moving to Market Harborough where he died in 1969 after a long illness. In the preface to the last edition of his *'History in Leicester'*, published after his death, appropriately was written: 'This work remains a fine memorial to a man who cared a great deal for and gave so much of his time and energy to the city of his birth'.

The second son of Bernard and Isabel, Oliver, was a flight sub-lieutenant in the Royal Navy Air Service, and was presumed killed in action in 1917. Before this he had attended Bootham School, York where he literally made his mark — not only as a fearless footballer, brilliant gymnast and naturalist (photographing the hatching of a cuckoo's egg) with great imaginative and literary gifts, but in 1916 by a daring escapade. For a challenge, Oliver, one night, climbed by hand and foot the outside of the huge North Eastern Railway offices in York and painted large white lettering on the roof. This was reported to the military authorities who thought it was a code to raiding German aircraft. In the inquiry Oliver owned up, but it was not believed anyone could carry out such a difficult climb until it was revealed he had painted his own initials. He died only a few months later in France.[52]

The family's youngest son, Richard, read medicine at Cambridge and after qualifying undertook relief work in Spain during the Spanish Civil War. He became a professor of Child Health and wrote three leading books on the subject.

Douglas Ellis 1861-1912

The 1881 census shows Douglas as a gardener aged 19, but after a brief spell working for Joseph Ellis & Sons in Birmingham, he was employed by Ellis & Everard as district manager at Hitchin. He became director of both companies and lived at Hitchin, where he married and had one son, Norman Douglas, in 1903.

He died at the age of 51, and as this was a year before his mother's death, was unfortunate not to receive her legacy of *Hayfield Farm* estate at Aspley Guise, Bedfordshire.

Douglas's son, Norman Douglas, joined Ellis & Everard in 1924 and for a short time worked at Peterborough and Hitchin. He became a director and secretary of the Ellis companies and was chairman of Ellis & Everard from 1963 to 1971.

He was also the first chairman (1946-1948) of the Institute of Corn and Agricultural

Merchants, and chairman of the council of the Leicester Charity Organisation Society. By 1954 he was a Leicester magistrate (and chairman of the magistrates for 9 years), he was chairman, and later president of the Leicester Trustee Savings Bank and director of the Leicester Permanent Building Society until 1974, when he moved to London. He was awarded the OBE for his work as local chairman of the Soldiers', Sailors' & Airmen's Family Association and other social causes. For most of his life he lived at *Brookland*, Meadowcourt Road, Oadby and died in 1991.

Norman Douglas Ellis, 1903-1991.

Norman Douglas had two sons, James Douglas and Anthony Norman (Bob). Bob joined Ellis & Everard Ltd and became a director in 1963. He was Group Property director, based in Newport Pagnell, and managing director of Ellis & Everard (Building Supplies) Ltd. When this division was taken over by Travis & Arnold in 1978 he moved to the new company, and he now lives in Oxfordshire.

John Shipley Ellis (Junior) 1865-1951

Whilst a young man at *Knighton Hall*, John Shipley Ellis took a world sailing tour to help cure a lung complaint and on his return in 1882, went to work at Ellis & Everard's district office in Peterborough. He was eventually chairman of the company from 1943 to 1951. He had three children, Margery Shipley, Jane Shipley and, in 1907, Francis John Shipley. He was a local

John Shipley Ellis Jnr, 1865-1951, of Leicester.

magistrate and, at the age of 50, joined the army during the First World War. He lived most of his life in Peterborough where he died aged 86. His elder daughter, Margery Shipley, was also a JP and awarded an MBE.

His son, Francis John Shipley Ellis, joined Ellis & Everard in 1928 and became a director in 1932. After he married Mary Isabella Legh Evans, twins Susan Legh and John Edward Shipley were born in 1931. A further son, George Henry was born in 1935, but died at only 18 when an officer cadet. Francis (known as John) lived most of his life at Elton near Peterborough and was a member of the Territorial Army, becoming a captain in the Royal Artillery during the Second World War. He was High Sheriff for Cambridgeshire, Huntingdonshire and Isle of Ely in 1962, and became deputy chairman of Ellis & Everard prior to his retirement in 1966. He moved to Norfolk and died in 1980.[53]

Twin, John Edward Shipley Ellis, moved to Leicestershire to work for the family companies living at Botcheston, Broughton Astley, Queniborough Old Hall and Stoneygate. He progressed within the group and became the Ellis & Everard group secretary until 1973. A former parish councillor, he lives in Buckinghamshire where he was once Mayor of Milton Keynes.

JAMES ELLIS MP 1829-1901

After a Quaker education at the renowned Ackworth School, Yorkshire (of which he later became a manager) and at Hitchin, James moved in 1853 from his first home at *Glenfield Lodge* to run his own farm called *Blue Pots* in Kirby Muxloe.[54] The farmhouse was leased from James Goode and was at the side of the newly-opened Leicester & Burton railway line (adjacent to the present Towers Close). Strangely, it was once an alehouse and at the time of James' occupation part of it was used as a temporary station booking office. The booking clerk, Job Grant, was also the stationmaster, signal man and porter, and was even employed by James' father to manage the adjacent Joseph Ellis coal wharf.

James Ellis, 1829-1901, of Kirby Muxloe and The Gynsills. (LMARS)

By 1860, however, James had moved to another of James Goode's properties on the south side of the 80 acres he was farming. It was called *Kirby Lodge*, but was renamed *Forest Edge* during James' occupation. It was situated near to the *Red Cow* public house in Leicester Forest East.[55]

In 1855 James married Louisa Burgess from the Quaker family at *Wigston Grange*, and in the next year the first of four boys and two girls was born. A year later he became a partner in both of the family firms, Joseph Ellis & Sons and Ellis & Everard. From then on farming was only a sideline, although, following his major part in setting up granite quarries for Ellis & Everard at Bardon Hill, he was to oversee the running of the surplus farmland there. In this area he often enjoyed game shooting with business partner, Breedon Everard, and he was also a keen fisherman.

Fortunately, James kept a series of very informative diaries and from those which remain, entries in 1857 show that he spent much time redesigning the steam-driven crushing plant installed at Bardon Hill.[56] The following year he and brother, Joseph Henry, were granted a patent for the designs that greatly advanced granite crushing techniques.[57]

Whilst living at Kirby Muxloe, James' innovative nature was shown again when he successfully experimented with balancing mixes of fertilizers and artificial manures to suit various crops — the final products sold to farmers through the Joseph Ellis and Ellis & Everard depots. Sales were good, and so with Joseph Henry he set up a processing plant in 1867. It was situated only two miles from his home near to Desford railway junction between Ratby and Newtown Unthank and the manager appointed was the versatile Job Grant, the booking clerk from *Blue Pots*!

James also left the Kirby Muxloe farm in 1867 (maybe he was too near the odorous processing plant) to live for a short time in *Glenfield House*, which had been vacated by his four sisters. This was followed by a move to *Glenfield Grange*, a house he was to call *The Gynsills*.[58] This still remains near to the corner of Groby Road and the road to Anstey and was next to *Anstey Grange*, the property of his cousin, William Henry Ellis.

A governor of the Wyggeston Hospital Schools, James also carried on the family tradition of promoting education for the less privileged. He was involved with the local school boards many of which were set up throughout England in the 1870s after the passing of the Elementary Education Act. He was on the Leicester School Board from 1879, was its chairman from 1884 to 1897 and was also chairman of the Anstey Board. In summer months the Ellises were often hosts to schoolchildren from Glenfield and Anstey who were treated to teas on the lawn at *The Gynsills*. In connection with the school boards, James was

The Gynsills at Glenfield, residence of James and later Herbert Ellis. It is now a public house and hotel.

instrumental in setting up the Desford Industrial School near Botcheston, which was designed primarily to teach agriculture. He was chairman of the managers from the school's inauguration in 1881 until his death, and with his farming expertise spent much time overseeing its development. Most of the school's produce was sold at Leicester market.[59]

Although initially having no involvement with politics, he helped Thomas T.Paget fight Parliamentary seats for South Leicestershire between 1867 and 1880, and with his interest fuelled, James himself stood as a Liberal candidate in 1885 for the first ever seat of the newly-created constituency of Bosworth (when South Leicestershire was divided into Harborough and Bosworth). He was elected that year (at the same time as his nephew, John Edward Ellis, entered Parliament) and was also successful in the election called the following year, attending the House until 1892. His main platforms were universal, free education and Home Rule, but he was generally disillusioned with Parliament, stating that there was too much debate and too little action to suit his own straightforward manner.

He was, however, occupied in many other spheres: he was chairman of the Leicester Savings Bank, director of Pares's Leicestershire Banking Company, chairman of the Leicestershire Liberal Association, vice-president of the Free Land League and a county magistrate from 1890. That year also, saw him became chairman of Ellis & Everard, leading the company until retiring through ill health in 1899. He died two years later, aged 71, after an amazingly energetic life, leaving his widow, Louisa, at *The Gynsills* until she died in 1913.

All four sons joined the family businesses, but the youngest, Alexander, lived for a few years in Australia before becoming auditor of both Ellis companies from 1899 to 1910. He died aged 50 in 1912. The other sons were with the companies far longer.

Herbert Ellis 1856-1922

Herbert Ellis, 1856-1922, of Leicester and The Gynsills. (LMARS)

Following the tradition of many members of the family, Herbert combined his business life with much public service.[60] After a Quaker schooling in York and then studying chemistry in Manchester, he became a partner in the two family-owned companies for which he worked all his life, including 18 years as company secretary for Joseph Ellis & Sons. He married American-born Alice Shipley Burgess in 1879 living at 62 New Walk, Leicester (then comprising mostly residential properties) followed by 112 and 120 Regent Road. They had a son and two daughters.

Herbert was chairman of the board of governors for Wyggeston Hospital for 17 years — for which a plaque in his honour is displayed inside the hospital chapel — and served in the same capacity for the Wyggeston schools for 6 years. He was governor of Alderman Newton's School, was a member of the management committee of his old school in York and taught at the Quaker Adult Schools for over 30 years.

A Leicester councillor from 1891 to 1899, he served on several of their committees and was a trustee of the Town Charities. He was secretary, and in 1906-7, the annual president of

The ceremonial key used to open Ellis Park, Glenfield in 1951.

the Leicestershire Literary & Philosophical Society and secretary of the Glenfield Land Society. He was also a county JP.

In business, he was chairman of Ellis & Everard from 1907, chairman of Leicester engineers, Taylor, Taylor & Hobson and a member of the management committee of St Martin's Bank. He was chairman of the Leicester commissioners of income tax and also auditor of the Leicester Permanent Building Society. With interests in a land company in Louisiana and Texas, and because of his family connections there, he was a frequent traveller to the United States.

On the death of his mother in 1913 he returned with Alice and daughters Valeria Dean and Hilda Margaret (who was president of the Leicester Girls' Social Guild) to live at his childhood home of *The Gynsills*. To reach his office in Leicester from there he would walk to catch a train at Glenfield station, always looking very distinguished in morning dress and silk topper. As in his early years at *The Gynsills*, the grounds of the estate were often open to the public for such occasions as the Adult School celebrating their anniversaries with a sports day, grand tea and evening dance.

Herbert died at the house in 1922 and, despite still being a Quaker, was buried in Glenfield churchyard. Alice died some 23 years later. The estate was then sold and the house occupied privately for about 40 years before conversion into a public house and hotel which is still called *The Gynsills*.

In memory of the family's long association with Glenfield, Herbert's two daughters, Valeria and Hilda, and their cousin, Maud (daughter of James Bancroft Ellis) gave the necessary funds for the building of Ellis Park and bowling green situated off Stamford Street. They opened it in June 1951. Appropriately, the park can be reached from Ellis Close and the Ellis name is also remembered in Glenfield with the naming of an electoral ward.

Theodore Burgess Ellis 1860-1942

Theodore Burgess Ellis, 1860-1942, of Leicester.

Educated like his elder brother at York and Manchester, Theodore similarly had a long record of work in education.[61] He taught for 38 years at the Quaker's Adult School Movement, firstly at their Soar Lane School, but after this was sold in 1895 for the impending Great Central Railway, he moved to their other school in Pike Street and then to a new one built between Short Street and Church Gate. Here he became president, a position he also held at the Leicestershire Adult School Union. He was on the committee of the Desford Industrial School for over 30 years and sat on the Leicester School Board until it was replaced in 1903 by the Education Committee of which he was a co-opted member.

A director of the Leicester Permanent Building Society for over 30 years (and chairman for two) he was also chairman of Harpers Cycle Co Ltd, of James Thomson & Co (Kendal) and Bardon Hill Quarries Ltd. This last concern was a sister company of Ellis & Everard for which Theodore started working in 1877 and became secretary and a director. He was also a director of Joseph Ellis & Sons.

For 39 years he was chairman of the Leicester District Nursing Association and for many years vice president of the Leicester Charity Organisation Society. He married Sarah Smithson who, like Theodore, became a magistrate. They lived most of their lives at *Crossways*, Stoneygate Road (now replaced by apartments) and at *Cartmel Close*, Stoughton Drive South. Sarah died in 1939 and Theodore in 1942.

James Bancroft Ellis 1861-1911

After attending the same schools as his elder brothers, James Bancroft was also involved, though to a lesser extent, in the Adult School Movement at Leicester and at Anstey and Glenfield. He was also on the Anstey School Board. He was secretary at Joseph Ellis & Sons and managed their Wigston branch, but was still able to carry out quite an unusual role. This was the secretaryship for England of the precisely named Louisiana & Southern States Real Estates & Mortgage Company, working from the Joseph Ellis head office at East Street. By 1890 he was travelling regularly in this post to the United States continuing until his death when cousin, Bernard Ellis, took over the position.

James Bancroft lived in Daneshill Road, Leicester with wife Ethel Sara until about 1902 when, as a country-loving gentleman (and a brilliant fruit grower), he moved to *The Cedars* in Glenfield Frith. This large property, at least 200 years old, was once owned by his father's cousin, Edward Shipley Ellis, as part of his large estate at Glenfield. Eventually the house was demolished in about 1964 and replaced by properties now situated in Cedars Close.

He had a daughter and one son, James Clive Ellis, who was taken prisoner during the First World War and died of wounds in a German field hospital aged 19.

A county councillor for Markfield for many years, James Bancroft was a member of the Leicester Distress Committee and secretary of the Leicester Charity Organisation Society. He died aged 51, his wife and daughter then moving to Leicester, firstly at New Walk and then at *Glenties*, Avenue Road, Stoneygate.

JOSEPH HENRY ELLIS 1831-1874

Joseph Henry was the youngest son of Joseph Ellis to be born at *Glenfield Lodge* farm, and strangely, according to the 1851 census, started his working life as a hosier's apprentice. By 1857, however, he was a partner in his father's merchandising businesses and was the first general manager over several Ellis & Everard depots at stations on the newly-opened Leicester & Hitchin railway. With his brother, James, he was instrumental in expanding both of the companies and the quarry business at Bardon Hill.

Joseph Henry Ellis, 1831-1874, of Stoneleigh.
(LMARS)

In 1860 he married Philadelphia-born Sarah Longstreth Thompson at the Hardshaw West Meeting House in Lancashire, a wedding notable for the marriage certificate that survives containing no less than 116 witnesses, although only five were signatures from the Ellis family.[62] Their first home was 37 London Road, Leicester, opposite the station, before moving to a house specially built for them in 1871 at Stoneygate Road. This was a huge, beautifully-designed house in stone called *Stoneleigh*.

At the time of the move Joseph Henry was a member of the borough council, having won seats in 1867 and 1869, and was elected again in 1872. He served on the board of health and, as an extremely capable and popular councillor, was elected alderman in 1873 (replacing his cousin Edward Shipley Ellis). Shortly after, however, he suffered from peritonitis and died in 1874 aged only 42. Among the large attendance of the funeral at Welford Road cemetery was the Mayor of Darlington, Arthur

Stoneleigh, Stoneygate Road, Leicester, built for Joseph Henry and his American wife, Sarah, in 1871. It is now divided into luxury apartments.

Pease, from the renowned Quaker family that had founded the Stockton & Darlington Railway.

Sarah continued to live at *Stoneleigh* with their three children, Gertrude (writer of a history of the Leicester Ladies Reading Society of which she was long-term president), Susan Morris (secretary of both the county Girls' Friendly Society and RSPCA) and son, Francis Joseph, who died when only 20. Sarah died in 1920 having been a widow for 46 years and the daughters moved to Avenue Road. Just a few years later, *Stoneleigh* was adapted for use as a school for deaf and partially-sighted children, continuing in use until the early 1980s when the building was converted into luxury apartments. Still visible, high on the wall, are the original occupant's initials entwined in an elaborate plaque.

JOSEPH ELLIS'S FOUR DAUGHTERS and GLENFIELD MEETING HOUSE

Glenfield House in The Square, one of the homes of Joseph Ellis's 4 daughters.

For many years Joseph Ellis's four daughters, Mary, Hannah, Sarah Anne and Sophia lived together. They first moved from their family home at *Glenfield Lodge* farm in 1856 along with their ailing father (who died a few months later) to live at *Glenfield House*. This is a five-bay, three-storey building of 1790 that can still be seen on The Square in the centre of the village. At the rear were stables, reached through a gateway (which has since been bricked up) from where the sisters would frequently drive their governess cart. On occasions this was to the Friends' Meetings in Leicester.[63] The sisters made an impact in the village, poorer people benefitting from their benevolence, and the local school is known to have received regular 'treats' from them like excursions in brakes to Bradgate Park.

Glenfield House was very near to a building known as the 'Meeting House'. This two-storey building (eventually used for various kinds of shop including a post office) had a prominent end wall of stone facing The Square. It is considered to be the building once owned by Quaker, Richard Hashold, who had used part of the property himself for a malting business (he is described in deeds as a maltster and mealman) before moving to Leicester in 1818. On leaving, he donated it to the Society of Friends for their meetings and to maintain a small, old burial ground nearby. Also on the site were a barn, warehouse and stables.

The number of Quakers in the village would have been few, but one of their members was Joseph Ellis who may even have boarded in the building many years earlier before taking up the farm at *Glenfield Lodge*. In 1854, and probably earlier, Joseph was renting at least part of the building from the 'Society of Quakers' for £14 a year, most likely for his malting business in succession to Richard Hashold.

By 1863 the property was in the name of his eldest daughter, Mary (who also owned three other houses and six-and-a-half acres of land in the village) and in 1866 its title was held by all four sisters. By 1882 it was in the

The Meeting House, Glenfield before demolition in 1994. (Glenfield Gazette)

name of their brother, James Ellis of *The Gynsills*, who is known to have attended meetings there (although none were held after 1887).[64] The building survived until 1994 when it was replaced by a housing development approached by a new road called The Maltings.

Only one sister married — Sarah Anne — who married Alfred Shipley in 1867 and lived in Bristol. At the same time, the other three sisters left Glenfield to live at 1 Westbourne Terrace, Leicester (now 17 Fosse Road Central) a very large end terrace in stylish polychrome brickwork. They were there for nearly 20 years before moving again in about 1887 to a large house in Blaby village called *The Limes*. This stood alone in nearly three acres of land on the north side of Enderby Road.

Hannah Ellis, 1832-1919, second daughter of Joseph Ellis. She was an artist and woodworker. (LMARS)

Hannah was the most enterprising sister and devoted much of her time to botany, watercolour sketches and writing. She was also adept at carpentry — often making toys, household items and wood carvings. With Sophia (also a keen painter) she helped set up the Leicester School of Art in the 1860s, one of her pupils being Eliza, a cousin from *Belgrave Hall*. Jointly with another cousin, Charlotte, Hannah was also secretary to the Leicester Charity Organisation Society and when in Blaby she ran the village library.

All three sisters died at Blaby, Sophia in 1898, Mary in 1901 and Hannah, who left her wealth to 18 different charities, in 1919. *The Limes* survives, now a hotel called *Time Out*, although part of its land had been sold earlier for a development around Lime Grove.

JOSEPH ELLIS & SONS LTD and
ELLIS CHEMICAL COMPANY LTD

Records show that the Joseph Ellis company was started in 1839, but did not trade until the following year.[65] This was when coal was sold from wharves rented at Countesthorpe and Ullesthorpe on the newly built Leicester to Rugby section of the Midland Counties Railway. Initially, coal from the Leicester—Swannington line was carted from West Bridge across the town to the new line at Leicester station, but it was soon realised that it was simpler to receive rail-borne coal directly along the Midland Counties line from Derbyshire. It is very likely that this coal came from George Stephenson's Clay Cross mine, a company that was already employing Joseph to tranship coal into canal barges at Rugby for destinations in the south. (Coal was never sold in Leicester as, by agreement, this was the domain of John Ellis & Sons.)

However, with Joseph Ellis preoccupied with many other business interests, the company did not expand for a further ten years when a depot was opened at Kirby Muxloe on the Leicester—Burton line. It was next to the *Blue Pots* farm which Joseph's son, James, was then occupying. Two outlets followed on the same railway and two on the Rugby & Stamford line, but it was James who really expanded the business along with brother, Joseph Henry, when, in the early 1850s, they opened branches in the Birmingham area. (Depots that the company opened, including ones taken over from other merchants, are listed in appendix IV.)

George Hickin, 80 years old, and Hayfield Charlie, 20 years old, about to make a delivery from Highgate Wharf, Birmingham in 1899.

DEPOTS:
WEST BRIDGE, LEICESTER.
COUNTESTHORPE.
BROUGHTON ASTLEY.

MIDLAND RAILWAY.

K. MARTIN,
District Manager

Goods forwarded to any Station.

LEICESTER DISTRICT.

Warehouse, WEST BRIDGE WHARF,
Order Office, St. AUGUSTINE STREET, WEST BRIDGE,
Central Office, EAST STREET, LONDON ROAD,

LEICESTER,

189

The Sparkenhoe Corn Flour Co

Bought of JOSEPH ELLIS & SONS, Ltd.

MANUFACTURERS OF

ARTIFICIAL MANURES FOR GRASS, CORN, ROOTS, &c.

DEALERS IN

Linseed Cake, Cotton Seed Cake, Maize, Rice Meal, Peruvian Guano, Salt, Nitrate of Soda, Soot, Silver Sand, Peat, Cocoa Nut Fibre, Stone, Gravel, American and Fine Flour, Oats, Beans, Peas, Barley Meal, Sharps, Bran, Hay, Straw, Peat Moss Litter, and Coal Bags.

Samples of bill headings used in the Leicester and Birmingham areas, 1897 and 1902.

Registered Offices :—10, EAST STREET, LEICESTER.

JOSEPH ELLIS & SONS, LIMITED,

BIRMINGHAM AGENCY.

COAL MERCHANTS.

DEPÔTS:
HIGHGATE WHARF (MID.)
KING'S HEATH „   „
NORTHFIELD „   „
STOKE WORKS „   „
HAGLEY ROAD „ (L. & N.W.)

MANAGER :—THOMAS SPIERS.

Highgate Wharf,
Birmingham.
Jany 31st 1902

They also increased the company's range of merchandise. In particular, fertilisers were sold in the rural areas, barge-loads and truck-loads of products such as imported guano and nitrate of soda being brought to West Bridge and stored in a new warehouse for distribution. Since 1849, when the Leicester—Burton line opened with a connection to the Leicester—Swannington line at Desford, it had been possible to receive a wide range of loads by rail at West Bridge as well as by canal and then forward mixed loads of goods to the various depots. With the expanding railway system there was a marked effect on the prosperity of farms and market gardens, which were able to receive new products via the trackside outlets as well as despatch their own goods to a wider market. This included selling grain to Joseph Ellis & Sons to either produce animal feeds or sell on to millers and maltsters.

With Breedon Everard, Joseph Ellis had also set up the Ellis & Everard company in 1848 which ran similar types of depots. His two companies were run in parallel, with members of the Ellis family sharing the senior management and, from 1857 (the year Joseph Ellis died) the companies also shared a head office. The first was at 44 Granby Street (since renumbered 54), and subsequently there were moves to 29 Granby Street in 1865, to 1 East Street in 1879 and 10 East Street in 1898. Although some things were shared, particularly in bulk buying, the finances were always kept separate, an arrangement which was to last for over 100 years.

Under the head office were district offices, which in turn controlled the depots through district managers.

During the second half of the nineteenth century the Joseph Ellis company was under the management of sons of a successful farmer and as such, the farmer's requirements were well known and well catered for. With the depots serving many farms and country estates, animal feeds had been successfully introduced to the range of merchandise. Many varieties of cattle cake were imported and their own feeds were manufactured at West Bridge for which grist mills and oat crushing plants were installed. By 1920 similar machinery had been installed at most of the major depots. The 'Speedwell' brand was set up to market several types of animal feed which proved popular for many years.

A boost to the sale of fertilizers resulted from the opening of the company's own manufacturing plant in 1867, situated conveniently by the railway with special sidings between Kirby Muxloe and Desford. It was called the Sparkenhoe Manure Works, company literature oddly showing its address as Glenfield. Superphosphates and varieties of bone-meal compounds were manufactured, and balanced, artificial manures to suit nearly all types of farm and garden crops were blended and mixed. The plant was successfully operative for over 60 years, but eventually large, specialist companies at the ports were able to manufacture most of its products more economically. The company's own brands of 'Sparkenhoe' fertilizers continued to flourish however.

An interesting aside about the works is the rather dangerous method employed to get mail on its way to the head office in Leicester and other offices along the line. It was permitted for letters to be handed from the trackside to the drivers of goods trains as they passed at about 25 miles per hour at the rear of the works. This occurred almost up to the time of the works closing in 1929 when the premises were sold to waste merchants, Berridge & Sons.

From the 1850s building materials were also introduced to most branches. Eventually, a very comprehensive range was available — for example, over 40 styles of chimney pot were offered in one sales catalogue. As with all products, they were stocked at depots according to demand; town depots stocking very different lines to (say) a small country depot selling just coal, lime and animal feed from a small store. There were also some unusual lines. At Highgate in Birmingham (where the company had private sidings) straw ropes were manufactured for packing bedsteads, and elsewhere soot was resold to market

There were many country stations with small warehouses serving farmers and remote villages. Typical was the one extant at Rothley on the Great Central Railway.

gardeners, having first been purchased from town chimney sweeps. Bulbs were imported directly from Holland for sale along with a vast range of seeds, rose plants and other garden products. At the start of the motoring era even petrol was sold — straight from the can — and various lubricants. Over the years, diversification of merchandise from the main line of coal proved very useful. With every household and business burning the product, there was plenty of competition from other merchants.

In 1893 the firm became a limited liability company, and because of general expansion, extra warehousing was taken at West Bridge including occupation of the original railway station. There was a further warehouse and stables purchased in Marble Street in 1912, and here was housed the company's first lorry — a conversion of a London taxi. Part of the building was also used to store products of the British Dyestuffs Corporation (later a founder member of ICI). This company contracted Joseph Ellis & Sons to deliver their dyes to the local textile trade and on the rounds it was found that there was a demand for the supply of other chemicals. Joseph Ellis & Sons were able to meet this demand and, coupled with promises of quick deliveries at the right price, a new business was created. At this time no-one could have predicted where this small step was to lead in the following 85 years!

So successful was the venture initially, that in 1915 a separate company was formed — the Ellis Chemical Co Ltd — which shared the head office at 10 East Street. Steady progress was then made, including during the wartime years, until 1951 when, under new management, there was rapid expansion and a new office opened at 65 London Road. Hosiery and allied trades were the biggest customers, but their large range of products was also sold to the local leather, polish, rubber, hat, laundry and electrical trades. In 1960 a distribution depot was opened at Pinfold Road, Thurmaston and the small London Road office closed. The company was run as a subsidiary of Joseph Ellis & Sons.

Meanwhile, between the wars, the amount of rail-side depots — once standing at almost 40 — was gradually reduced as delivery lorries began to replace horses and carts. The smaller country outlets were closed, but with the improved efficiency, business showed a marked increase. At Hinckley, for example, from managing with two horses, eventually 39 lorries were required. The only increase in branches was when companies were taken over such as at Leamington Spa with Cox's coal business in 1927 and Alline Wayte's corn business in 1932.

By the 1950s and 60's, however, the demand for domestic and industrial coal, forage and agricultural products had declined, and with the start of the Beeching cuts of branch lines, the number of depots was reduced further. For the company to prosper it was necessary to concentrate more on the chemical trade and on the expansion of the building supplies for which the main depots were then at Hinckley, Coalville, Leicester, Rugby, Nuneaton and Leamington. For this, capital was required. The situation was similar at Ellis & Everard Ltd, and so in the early 1960s it was decided that floatation was the way forward. Firstly, it was necessary to amalgamate the two companies which, in effect, meant that Joseph Ellis & Sons Ltd was absorbed by the larger Ellis & Everard. Listing on the stock exchange followed in December 1963 and the necessary funds were raised, but it was to mark the end of the Joseph Ellis company that had maintained its independence as a family concern for 124 years.

ELLIS & EVERARD LTD

From about 1844 Joseph Ellis and farmer Breedon Everard from Groby (brother of brewery pioneer, William Everard) were both employed to negotiate for land during construction of the new Syston & Peterborough railway. However, they were probably well acquainted before this as their farms were only one-and-a-half miles apart. Unlike Joseph, Breedon is not mentioned in the railway's construction committee minutes, so maybe he played only a minor role. Near to completion of their railway work, though, they were both equal partners when, showing their enterprising spirit, they opened coal and lime depots at most of the stations on the line.[66] Quite large towns were served — Stamford, Oakham, Peterborough and Melton — where outlets were opened in 1848. The Ellis & Everard company was thus established and further depots were opened, many on the new Leicester & Hitchin line in 1857 and on the Peterborough to Wisbech

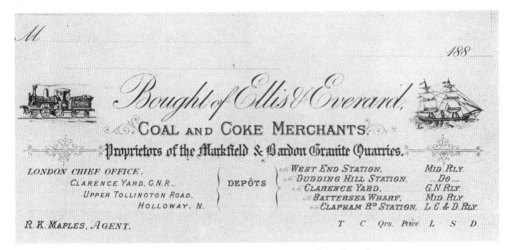

Ellis & Everard had various depots in the London area as this 1880s bill heading shows.

line ten years later. There were subsequent openings and acquisitions of depots on many other lines, including some in London, until at one time there were well over 60 depots in operation. They were nearly all to the east and south of Leicestershire (see list of depots in appendix IV) whilst those of Joseph Ellis & Sons were quite separate and mostly to the west of the county.

The main commodity sold was coal which, prior to the depots opening, had been brought to the area from the north by sea to the east coast ports and then up the rivers Ouse, Nene and Welland. Other items were soon offered, mostly building materials and agricultural items, much the same as at the outlets of Joseph Ellis & Sons, and very often the price lists and catalogues were shared. Also shared were stands at numerous county agricultural shows, although of the three Royal Shows held in Leicester in 1868, 1896 and 1924, they exhibited only at the first.

One commodity that Ellis & Everard sold in large quantities was granite. This came from their own quarry at Bardon Hill and sold very well for road making, particularly in East Anglia. Timber was another important line at some depots and eventually a lime-spreading service was offered. From a warehouse near Wisbech docks, certain imported items like French slates and American and continental cattle feed were distributed. Other animal feeds were made at their own larger depots and artificial fertilizers were purchased from Joseph Ellis's 'Sparkenhoe' works.

As well as Joseph's many descendants working for the company, Breedon Everard's son,

Still the most common delivery method in the 1930s – at Crescent Wharf, Peterborough.

Charles, was also a partner from 1880. In succession, his son, Charles Miskin and finally his two sons, Anthony and Simon all became chairmen of this truly family concern that became a limited company in 1890.

A reflection on how the business expanded during its first 100 years can be seen from the changes in transport and number of depots as shown in the following table taken from the company's centenary book:

	1851	1873	1898	1923	1947
Railway Wagons	14	196	236	232 and 140 hired	-
Horses (heavy)	6	24	62	70	12
Horses (driving) & ponies	-	5	6	-	-
Motor Lorries	-	-	-	10	117
Electric Lorries	-	-	-	-	3
Motor Vans	-	-	-	-	2
Motor Cars	-	-	-	6	19
Motor Bicycles	-	-	-	8	2
Pedal Bicycles	-	-	-	16	5
Total number of stations kept as separate depots	14	41	50	58	43
Depots with horses or lorries	4	19	23	29	36

The railway wagons in the list were first purchased in 1848 for the Syston & Peterborough line, all of the wagons at that time, and for a few more years, of the unsprung-buffer type. Although they broke more easily, this type were not completely phased out until as late as 1914. There were no wagons owned in 1947 as they were compulsorily taken over during the war and

One of Ellis & Everard's first motor lorries standing in the Market Place, Wisbech in the early 1920s. It appears to be an entrant in a parade.

bought by British Railways at nationalisation. From the figures for 1947 it can be seen that most of the horses had been replaced by lorries with a resulting decrease in depots. The last delivery by horse and cart was in 1956. Not shown on the list are the narrow boats owned by the company when Market Harborough coal merchant, West & Ellis (unrelated), was taken over in 1920. They were used for industrial coal and the only known names of the boats were *Evelyn, Enid and Arthur*.[67]

Between the Wars, the familiar '4 Es' sign and the company's standard red lettering was first used. They became a regular sight to those who lived in or travelled by train through the trading areas. The '4 Es' sign, used until 1978, was developed from a swastika symbol (with no German connections) that had previously been used on company letter headings.

Virtually from the company's beginning right up to the Second War there had been continued growth for most years in all sectors. However, towards the 1950s, due to the increasing competition from more convenient sources of power — oil, gas and electricity —the coal trade declined. With this, and the agriculture trade being less profitable at the time, the number of depots was reduced considerably. Development then tended to be away from the railways and concentrated on the builders' merchant's trade. As mentioned with the Joseph Ellis

Old and current corporate signs ('4 Es' and '2 Es') of Ellis & Everard Ltd.

company, Ellis & Everard Ltd was floated in 1963 inheriting the Joseph Ellis outlets and the all-important Ellis Chemical Company. On the new board, the family members were Colin D.B.Ellis (Chairman), Francis John S.Ellis, Norman D.Ellis, Anthony N.Ellis, Anthony J.Everard and Simon Everard. The first three named all retired between 1965 and 1971, leaving a sound and successful company. At the time of the stock

One of hundreds of the company's private owner wagons. Livery was predominantly red. (Historical Model Railway Society)

market floatation, sales were: Building — £2.5m, Agriculture — £2.5m, Coal — £2.3m and Chemical Distribution — £0.2m.

Two years before floatation, the company moved from their head office in East Street, where redevelopment was to take place, to improved premises purchased at 140-142 New Walk, which had previously been the *Cravenhurst Hotel.*

The decision was then made to form three separate divisions within the company, namely Building Supplies & Fuel, Chemicals and Agriculture. Parts of the diminishing fuel trade were sold, while some parts were traded under Welland Fuels Ltd and others as Kee Fuels Ltd after a merger with Hercock-Simpson Ltd in 1971. For the building supplies, radical improvements were made to a number of existing properties and new businesses acquired. A result of this was that a comprehensive range of merchandise was formed with the development of the lighter side of the trade — ironmongery, electrical and plumbing materials — which was sold from retail counters at the major warehouses. This led to the self-selection departments including gardening, kitchen and bathroom equipment and the beginning of the do-it-yourself trade — quite a new departure in the early 1960s. By 1971 there were 29 of these major outlets situated in 11 counties throughout the Midlands and further south.

Meanwhile, the Ellis Chemical Company was rapidly expanding. Between 1964 and 1969 Charles Forth, Nottingham; WHB Chemicals, Bradford; Alfred Green, Northampton; A.W.Brook, Leicester; and Gould Thomas, Keynsham were purchased and in 1969 they were combined to form a separate company, Ellis & Everard (Chemicals) Ltd. In the following decade, after the group had fought off a takeover bid by Unilever, the company forged ahead with several

The Head Office in New Walk, Leicester. It was converted from the Cravenhurst Hotel in 1961. The Head Office moved to Bradford in 1988.

more acquisitions such that it was able to supply chemicals to all varieties of manufacturing, food and pharmaceutical industries throughout Britain. The only new development which never really succeeded was a leisure section created in 1978, mainly to install and maintain private swimming pools, trading as Capital Leisure Ltd.

Away from chemicals, the Agricultural Division proved to be the least profitable and so some parts of it were sold and the rest ceased trading in 1970. A recession in the building trade towards the end of the 1970s also led to some poor returns in the other division. This resulted in the entire building supplies business and remainder of the fuel trade being sold to Travis & Arnold Ltd (now Travis Perkins) in 1978. Anthony N.Ellis was head of this division and he moved on to Travis & Arnold. It marked the end of the Ellis family involvement with the company.

Partly from the proceeds of these sales and a 30% stake in the company taken by ICI (most of which it held until 1991) the chemicals side was able to expand beyond recognition. Led by Simon Everard, there were numerous acquisitions including the first in the United States in 1982 and three distributors that were able to cover the whole of Ireland in 1987. Ellis & Everard became the UK's largest distributor of chemicals. Group functions were, by then, centred on Bradford (where the computer centre was opened at *Ellis House* in 1983), and so in 1988 the Head and Registered Office was relocated there in Peckover Street. The Leicester office in New Walk was then closed, thus severing the ties with the city where the company had maintained its head office since 1857.

Another major step was taken in 1991 when the company entered into polymer distribution. Growth in this market saw the company selling in Europe as well as expanding their American

One of a large fleet of present-day lorries used for distributing chemical products throughout Britain.

trade. By the time this line really took off, Simon Everard had retired as chairman in 1994.

To give an idea of the overall growth of the chemical business (which, it is maintained, is all because of the 1915 maxim used at the start of their business 'to deliver the required product at the right time at the right price') the following table sets out the company's turnover at various periods:

Year	1915	1963	1970	1975	1977	1980	1985	1989	1995	1997	2001
Turnover £ million	.019	.20	2.41	7.50	14.99	28.20	88.30	215	514	645	900

This shows an incredible growth and at the beginning of 2001, as well as being the UK's largest distributor of chemicals and polymers and exporting to over 90 countries, the company was the third largest in America and the fourth largest in the world. All this came about through countless acquisitions and mergers that have occurred throughout the company's history, from small coal and corn merchants to large distributors of building materials and chemicals. With a small amount of irony therefore, although it all makes good business sense, Ellis & Everard plc were themselves taken over during 2001 by Dutch company, Royal Vopak, who now stand number one in the world. All this must have been beyond the wildest dreams of either of the two Leicestershire pioneers, Ellis and Everard, when they started the partnership in 1848. Fortunately, it is the intention of the holding company to retain these two names for trading in this country for the time being, although in North America the name Univar is now used.

BARDON HILL QUARRIES (ELLIS & EVERARD) LTD

Soon after their first trading on the Syston & Peterborough Railway, the successful partnership of Joseph Ellis and Breedon Everard continued when they purchased a granite quarry at Hall Lane, Markfield in 1852. They had realised the business potential of granite with its increasing use for road metalling at that time. For a few years previously Breedon had worked a small quarry on land that the family owned near to Billa Barra, one-and-a-half miles west of Markfield.

The Ellis & Everard quarry produced setts, kerbs and broken granite for macadamising and was operated independently of their merchandising businesses in Leicester. Up to 100 men were employed at Markfield, many for set dressing, but because of the many coalmines springing up in the area there was often a labour shortage. A row of 20 stone cottages was therefore provided for the workmen on Hillside, and these can still be seen.

Most of the quarry products were despatched by rail, but this entailed laborious carting for three-and-a-half miles along the A50 to Bardon Hill station. To increase efficiency in this journey, therefore, an ingenious cable haulage system was developed in the early 1870s by Breedon Everard's son, John Breedon.[68] He was a trained railway engineer who formed a civil engineering company with Samuel Pick that still operates in Leicester. Unfortunately, little is known about the system, but because of public opposition and the relatively small loads carried, it did not last long, and carting by road was continued right up to the time the quarry closed. This was, directories indicate, in the late 1920s — the time when granite setts had mostly been replaced by tarmacadam. The quarry was abandoned and it remains filled with water.

Only five years after Markfield was started, another quarry, much larger and more convenient for the railway, was opened by the partners in 1857. This was at Bardon Hill on land rented from the Hood family. With the death of Joseph Ellis, however, in that year, the partnership was run by two of his sons, James and Joseph Henry. They each had a quarter share in the business, whilst Breedon Everard had half.

Here, production soon grew. The granite was sold almost immediately in London, as well as at their own rail-side depots, and to save manpower a large, steam-driven crushing mill was purchased in 1858. It was the first to be used successfully in the country and the crushing techniques involved were continually improved. James Ellis put a lot of work into its development and even patented part of the design. As the granite was only suitable for roadstone and railway ballast rather than setts, all of the granite was crushed at this quarry and also some from Markfield (until a small crusher was installed there in 1892). The product was marketed as 'patent machine-broken granite' and larger and more powerful machinery was installed at Bardon in 1874 and 1902.[69]

An engraving of the first breaking mill at Bardon Hill depicted in an 1861 company catalogue.

Labour was still short and so the landowners, the Herricks of Beaumanor (who held the land title from 1864 to 1975 and drew royalties on the tonnage of rock produced) assisted with the provision of rows of cottages and a school room near to the quarry in the 1870s and 1890s. In 1890 there were 700 workmen employed, but by the start of the First World War, improved mechanisation had reduced that number by about a half. From the outset a standard gauge railway linked the quarry with the Midland Railway's Leicester to Burton line at Bardon Hill station (a connection which still runs across the main Coalville road) and within the quarry a 2ft-gauge railway was used until about 1960.

The huge Bardon Hill breaking mill taken c.1905. The first part was erected in the 1870s, doubled in size in 1902 and still stands.

A company catalogue of 1907 shows that 120 councils were regular customers of Ellis & Everard quarries which, by then, included a further production site situated near to Shepshed south of the Ashby road.

65

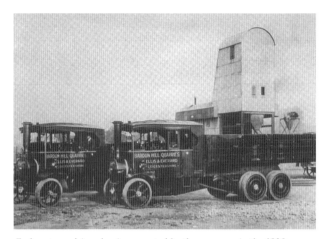

Foden steam-driven lorries operated by the company in the 1920s. (Greg Tom)

This was the Charnwood Granite Company which had been purchased in 1891 and produced mostly roadstone of a similar type to that at Bardon. Here, new crushing mills were set up and a standard gauge rail link installed which ran under the road near the quarry to join the London & North Western Railway's Charnwood Forest line half-a-mile away at Shepshed station. These lines were in use until 1963. For the internal workings at the quarry a 2ft-gauge rail system was also installed, this system lasting until about 1932. Later catalogues show that by the 1930s over 200 councils were among Ellis & Everard customers.[70]

Regarding ownership of the business, following the death of Breedon Everard in 1882, two of his sons, William Thomas and John Breedon, each held a quarter share. The latter then purchased half of the Ellis share, at that time held by James since Joseph Henry's death in 1874. Succeeding James as partner was Herbert Ellis in 1901 who, in turn, was succeeded in 1922 by Theodore Burgess Ellis — the last family member in the firm. He was the chairman when a limited company, Bardon Hill Quarries (Ellis & Everard) Ltd, was formed in 1930 — at that time one of the main producers of granite in the country. Four years before this, plant had been installed for the company to commence production of tarmacadam.

Business declined in the 1930s and the Shepshed site was sold in 1936. However, this quarry still operates having had various owners, including Amalgamated Roadstone, Amey Roadstone and Hanson Aggregates. At Bardon, the Second World War brought increased business, especially due to the construction of several military camps and airfield runways throughout Britain. It did mark the end, however, due to requisitioning, of the company's distinguished fleet of mainly yellow railway wagons which then totalled 214.

By 1948, the head of the company was Bernard Everard, son of John Breedon Everard and he was joined by Leonard Tom, a member of a family of quarry owners who purchased a large stake in the company and took a controlling interest in 1950. 'Ellis & Everard' was dropped from the title in 1969, a year when the annual output of Bardon Hill Quarries Ltd was 800,000 tons. Interesting comparisons are the figures from 1948 when only 58,000 tons were produced and 1890 when production was 175,000 tons.

With an increased diversity of products and services the company became the Bardon Group in 1977 and, following expansion with major acquisitions, was merged 20 years later to form the conglomerate, Aggregate Industries plc. This international company is based at Bardon, and it is interesting to reflect that a legacy of Joseph Ellis and Breedon Everard has now become one of Britain's super quarries where annual production is over three million tons. With its expansion, the rows of cottages – 80 dwellings in all – which formed a small village at the quarry, have had to be removed, the last occupants rehoused at the end of the 1980s.

SECTION 3
JAMES ELLIS
AND HIS IRISH CONNECTION

JAMES ELLIS
1793-1869

After his early life at *Sharman's Lodge* in Leicester Frith and education at Hartshill School, Warwickshire, James left the county of his birth for Yorkshire.[71] He was 15 and left to start an apprenticeship in corn milling with Quaker, Joshua Priestman at Thornton-le-Dale near Pickering. He worked there for six years, although for several weeks he was imprisoned as a conscientious objector, having been balloted for the militia, but insisted on upholding his faith, which disapproved of war.

In 1814 James moved to Hull to set up his own corn milling business and the following year he married Mary Priestman, daughter of his former employer. In the same trade he moved to Bingley in about 1822 and then, with his brother-in-law, John Priestman, the James Ellis & Company was established at the Old Soke Mills, Bradford.[72]

James Ellis, 1793-1869, of Yorkshire and Ireland. (LMARS)

At one time James' business had the monopoly of local malt sales from which he made large profits, but on becoming an ardent supporter of the temperance movement this part of the business was dropped. Financial losses were more than compensated for, however, when the partners also started in the worsted spinning trade, a business which proved very successful. In true family and Quaker tradition, some of the profits were given to education when a Ragged School was started for the poor on their own premises, and, with other members of the Society of Friends, another school for all denominations was started in 1830.

With a number of Yorkshire Quakers, James also helped to establish an insurance company, the Friends' Provident Institution, in 1832. James was a director until his death and was chairman on three occasions.[73] The company has grown ever since and now, with offices worldwide, Friends Provident plc is a leading life assurance and pensions company.

1832 was also a distressing year for James. His wife died, leaving him with five young children, but he did marry again, this time to Mary Wheeler of Hitchin in 1837. In this marriage one child was born, but died when very young.

The worsted business was very profitable, although, with his belief that 'the accumulation of riches was a snare to parents and a source of great injury to children' he decided, in 1848, to retire from business and devote his time and money to the benefit of others.

At this period there was great hardship for the poorer families in England, but in Ireland there was a far greater plight. Reports from fact-finding missions by the Quaker movement on the effects of the horrific potato famine there, and the necessity for relief work, reached James and Mary, and they decided to head for one of the worst affected areas, Connemara on Ireland's west coast. They moved there in 1849 when James was 56, and were soon established in a very small community at Letterfrack. They were joined by two of James' children, James Austin and Catherine.

For four years the famine had been taking its toll in the country with almost a million souls dying of hunger and disease in appalling conditions. The government's food aid was insufficient, and even their employment rates for the men still able to work on the likes of road and quay construction were below poverty level. Landlords were the other main employer and they exploited the labourers by paying irregularly and barely sufficient for a living to be made from the few jobs available.

At Letterfrack, James and Mary were able to import some food and with longer term considerations James leased 1,000 acres of land and employed many hands on various projects with sustaining rates of pay. Within his land, which was mostly mountain and bogland, he built a large, two-storey family home (within 5 months) and, employing over 80 men, he drained much of the area, eventually planting thousands of trees and constructing walls, gardens and roads. Also completed was a small school (for which he employed a schoolmaster) that doubled as a Meeting House, doctor's home and dispensary, shop and temperance hotel. All formed a village centre along with cottages of stone and slate for his employees. Near to the Ellis's house a variety of farm buildings were gradually added for the cattle, pigs and horses plus offices, barns and stores. The house was in an elevated position at the foot of the dominating Diamond Hill, and from its western aspect were magnificent views of the beautiful Connemara coastline. This provided some compensation for the more depressing human scenes.

In the first year James had organised the cultivation of all kinds of vegetables and a small quantity of wheat was sown. Varieties of fruit were also introduced (including strawberries 'that grow like weeds') and for all the produce, mixtures of composts using local peat, seaweed, lime and manure were tried and used to good effect. No doubt, he had remembered some of the farming techniques he must have seen in his early days on the family farm at Leicester Frith. He probably also recalled the times there when the family welcomed the popular Irish travellers who faithfully descended on the farm each summer to work on the harvest.

In Letterfrack, wife Mary also was very active, distributing money to urgent cases, giving out clothing sent from England, starting craftwork and being involved with the school and shop. She readily accepted her radical change from the comfortable standards in England and wrote in 1850: 'What we expended in Bradford, we find very well keeps our family and fifty others, leaving enough to educate one hundred and twenty children'.

At first there was suspicion and some adverse reaction to their work, both from other landlords and from the established church in Ireland, but Mary and James, after showing their

The start of the Ellis Wood Trail in Connemara National Park on Ireland's west coast.

political impartiality and belief in religious tolerance, were soon accepted, appreciated and encouraged. There were many adversities, of course, but in the first few years they both had a marked affect on the community and as a result of their efforts many lives were saved and standards of life generally improved. In some cases sufficient money was earned to achieve a life-long ambition — an emigration ticket to America. Although he gave relief to only a small part of the total population, it was a huge effort by one man.

Nearly eight years were spent in Letterfrack, and when James decided to leave it was only because of his failing health; he did not wish to risk leaving Mary a long way from her family and friends. It was with great reluctance they left as there was still work to be done and they had made many acquaintances. They returned to England with James' two children in 1857, leaving behind an excellent reputation and hope from their example.

James and Mary moved into *High Hall*, at Thornton-le-Dale near to where James had spent his first years in Yorkshire. Here, he recovered his health, but unfortunately became a widow once more when Mary died only six months after their return. He was cared for by the wife of his youngest son, James Austin, who had died aged 33 in 1860. (James' eldest son, Henry, had died at school when only 14.) Unusual was the life of his middle son, Joseph, who left the Quaker movement when he married a 'non-member' in 1850.[74] After finishing at Cambridge University, Joseph became a Church of England clergyman in Bradford, and

Ellis Hall, the community centre in Letterfrack.

published two pamphlets on religion. He was a regular correspondent with his cousin, Eliza, at *Belgrave Hall.*

At Thornton, James continued with local charity work whilst his health permitted, but after a long illness he died on 13 August 1869 and was buried at the Pickering Meeting House. He is especially remembered in Ireland: the Letterfrack community hall and the arts centre are named after him and the results of his planting 11,000 trees on his land now form a large wood within the Connemara National Park. From the park's visitor centre the 'Ellis Wood Trail' is a directed walk through marvellous scenery. The former Ellis house still stands high in the village and is now used as a youth hostel; the old Meeting House/schoolroom also remains nearby.

SECTION 4
ROBERT ELLIS AND DESCENDANTS

ROBERT ELLIS 1797-1873

Although raised with his three older brothers on the farm at *Sharman's Lodge*, Robert, as far as is known, did not have the same private education as they — maybe he was not as academic. He certainly did not lead such a high profile life.

Probably around the time the family gave up the tenancy of *Sharman's Lodge* in 1816, Robert left Leicester for Yorkshire, where he married Jane Coats of Adlington, near Hull, in 1818. The fact that she came from the Hull area indicates that Robert may well have moved near there to work with his brother, James, who had a milling business in the town.

Robert and Jane, however, settled in the West Riding at Bingley where, between 1820 and 1827, five children were born (although one died in infancy). Two years after the last was born tragedy struck with the death of Jane, and Robert was left a widower at the age of 32.

Robert Ellis, 1797-1873, of Yorkshire and Leicester. (LMARS)

During much of his time at Bingley he was possibly again working with James, who had moved his business to the area in 1822.

By 1840 Robert had returned to Leicester with his two sons, two daughters and a housekeeper — his sister-in-law Elizabeth Coats. They lived in Highcross Street, their property situated just north of All Saints Close and eventually numbered 164. Here, he ran a business as a maltster, corn, salt and flour dealer, initially in partnership with another brother, Joseph — although, because he was occupied in other fields, Joseph's involvement in the business was probably only to supply malt and grain from his Glenfield farm. From the Highcross Street premises, where he lived the rest of his life, Robert was also the Leicester agent for two insurance companies: Mutual Life Insurance and National Provident Institution, an offshoot of his brother James' Bradford company.

Like so many members of the family, Robert took up civic duties and was a borough councillor, elected continuously from 1850 to 1865. He was also elected alderman in 1861, from which he retired after ten years, and was on the Board of Guardians. He died aged 76 and was buried alongside family members at Welford Road cemetery.

Rather than follow in their father's business, his two sons, Frederick and John, together pursued an entirely different career of their own.

FREDERICK ELLIS 1825-1891, JOHN ELLIS 1827-1885 and F & J ELLIS LTD (GLOVE MANUFACTURERS)

John Ellis, 1827-1885, of Leicester.
(LMARS)

Both Frederick and John showed enterprise at the start of their working lives when, without previous experience, they started a glove manufacturing business.[75] This was about 1845 — the time when Leicester had the largest number of stocking frames of any town in the western world — and the design of many of these frames had been adapted to produce knitted products of various kinds including gloves.[76]

The type of knitting the brothers ventured into was quite specialised and was more profitable than hose; the pay was also better for the workers. There was a high demand for the product at the time and in the 1840s over a quarter of the 4,000 frames in Leicester were producing gloves. The brothers correctly assessed a reasonable future for their venture as the company, shown in directories as F & J Ellis from the 1860s, was in business for the next 120 years.

They started at a time when ownership of frames by cottage knitters was nearly at an end, and their arrangement was to lease out some of their own frames to home workers and operate others in a new factory. Their premises were in Rutland Street, next to the *Wellington Hotel*.

Possibly the last hand frame to be used in a Leicestershire factory for production work. This was taken in 1960 at F & J Ellis's Halkin Street factory.

A boost to the business occurred in 1887 when the glove making side of Richard Harris & Sons of King Street — one of the largest hosiery businesses in the country and in financial trouble at the time — was taken over, including machines, stock and personnel. All was set

up in a new branch in Pocklingtons Walk under the manager's name of James Gamble & Company. By far the firm's most successful product was taken over in the deal — 'Berlin' fine, white gloves of which, before the turn of the century, over four million pairs were sold to America alone. Later, other types did particularly well, being sold to the armed forces and to nearly every police force in the country.

The F & J Ellis factory in Rutland Street prior to the 1929 street widening.
(LMARS)

Although wider, powered frames were gradually introduced to the hosiery factories to produce fabric that could be 'cut up', hand-operated frames continued to be used by F & J Ellis for a long time. Outside framework knitters were employed until after the First World War, and in their factory a small number of frames were still being worked in the 1930s. These were used for special fancy gloves, and one frame, amazingly, was used in regular production into the 1960s. This was probably the last hand-operated frame in Leicestershire, although in Nottinghamshire a company was using frames to make shawls into the 1980s. After the First World War, F & J Ellis employed many outworkers and sub-contractors around the county using the company's much simpler flat bed and circular machines (still hand operated) and this system continued until closure.

After 84 years at Rutland Street, road widening had forced the factory to move, and premises were found in Halkin Street. This was 1929, and at the time of the move the firm became a limited company. In addition to Halkin Street and Pocklingtons Walk, the company also had premises in the late 1920s at Brookfield Street, Syston and, during the 1950s and 60s, a head office at 25 Friar Lane. However, like hundreds of other

Ernest Edward Ellis, 1856-1929, with wife Mary (in hat) and son, John Eric.
(LMARS)

hosiery companies in the area, a few also trading for well over 100 years, F & J Ellis was forced to close, mainly because of cheap imports prevailing from the early 1960s. All trading therefore ceased in 1967.

The company was a family concern from beginning to end. Co-founder, Frederick Ellis, who had lived in Conduit Street, *Cromwell House*, Humberstone Road and 2 West Walk, died in 1891 by which time one of his two sons, Robert Henry, was a partner. He lived at St James Road and then at South Street, Barrow-on-Soar (with his sister, Helena, a Guardian of the Poor) where he died in 1907.

The other founding partner, John, lived for some time in King Street and almost 20 years at *Pendean*, Avenue Road, Stoneygate. Like his brother, one of his sons, Ernest Edward became a partner. He lived mostly at *The Old Rectory*, Tilton-on the-Hill and one of his sisters, Henrietta, was a writer of small historical pieces.

The final member of the family to run the business was Ernest Edward's son, John Eric Ellis. He started with the company in 1908 and took control when his father died in 1929 just before the company moved to Halkin Street. He lived in Toller Road, Stoneygate for over 46 years until 1982.

POSTSCRIPT

The constraints of this book have been the Ellis's part in Leicester's history. It has examined the industry and good works of the many descendants of a father and son who wished to start a new life in Leicestershire at the end of the eighteenth century. Through their business enterprise they were able to add to the wealth of Leicester; but the family went beyond that in its concern for the welfare and education of the people. They were true public benefactors.

Their businesses, John Ellis & Sons, Ellis Partridge, Joseph Ellis & Sons, Ellis Chemical Company, Ellis & Everard and F & J Ellis grew and adapted to changing market conditions but, as almost invariably happens with such concerns, for various reasons the family connection cannot be maintained forever. This was true with all of these businesses, which were eventually subject to take-overs and closures, bringing about their end in the 1960s, 70s and 80s. These once familiar names disappeared from the local scene and it marked the end of Leicester's Ellis story.

There are many descendants of the four brothers around whom this book has been written; most have spread away from Leicester, and many have been very successful in their own chosen fields. They, no doubt, will be proud of their Quaker ancestors who contributed so much in a variety of ways to Leicester's past.

REFERENCES AND NOTES

Publications referenced are shown in the bibliography.
Abbreviations:
TLAHS   Transactions of the Leicestershire Archaeological & Historical Society
LRO   The Record Office for Leicestershire, Leicester & Rutland
PRO   Public Record Office, Kew

[1] Freeman Hardy & Willis, Olivers, Timsons and Stead & Simpsons are probably the best known.

[2] Dinah Freer, 'The Dynasty-builders of Victorian Leicester', *TLAHS*, Volume 53, 1978

[3] For details of this family see Shirley Ellis, *A Mill on the Soar*

[4] Charlotte Ellis, *Sketches of One Branch of the Ellis Family in Yorkshire and Leicestershire*; Margaret Ellis (compiled by), *Letters and Memorials of Eliza Ellis*. Both frequently used for the early history of the family.

[5] For other related families see Joan Johnson, *James and Mary Ellis*

[6] LRO 18D64/1

[7] G.E.Fussell, 'Four Centuries of Leicestershire Farming', *TLAHS*, Volume 24, 1948

[8] Each winter John Ellis purchased a cartload of Whitwick coal for his Beaumont Leys home. Maybe it was supplied by Whitwick colliery owner, William Stenson, and this was how they were acquainted.

[9] Hunter Davies, *George Stephenson, The remarkable life of the founder of railways*, p55

[10] Dr Ian Y.Ashwell, *John Ellis, Esq., Chairman of the Midland Railway Company*

[11] C.R.Clinker, *The Leicester & Swannington Railway*

[12] *Post Office Railway Directory* 1847

[13] PRO RAIL 384/41 minutes 553, 555

[14] Isabel C.Ellis (collected by), *Records of Nineteenth Century Leicester*, p70

[15] Edward H.Milligan, *Quakers and Railways*, p13

[16] Conjecture that the artist had depicted an LNWR engine emerging from the tunnel on what had become a Midland Railway branch line is untrue. The pose, with railway behind, was reminiscent of a famous portrait of George Stephenson also by John Lucas.

[17] D.A.Ramsey, *Newtown Linford Notes and the Leicestershire Slate Industry*

[18] F.T.Mott, *Charnwood Forest and Country Lodgings*

[19] A similar business was already being run successfully by John's brother, James, in Bradford.

[20] LRO DE2043 (A.M.Mackness, *Patons & Baldwins Ltd Story of West Bridge Mills Leicester 1839-1948*)

[21] Florence E.Skillington, 'The Coltmans of The Newarke at Leicester', *TLAHS*, Volume 18, 1935

[22] Isabel C.Ellis (collected by), *Records of Nineteenth Century Leicester*, p313; also, as secretary of 'The Association', Edward Shipley Ellis published a list in the *Leicester Chronicle*, 15 March 1856, of 33 master sweeps in the county who were complying with the Act of Parliament. For these people 'The Association' had purchased new 'machines' to replace the boys.

[23] Other partners were William Walker of Coleorton and William Paget of Sutton Bonnington. For early history of the mines see J.Beardsmore, *The History of Hucknall*.

[24] Between the time father and son were at the helm another Leicester man, W.E.Hutchinson, was in the chair from 1864-70.

[25] LRO 3D42/57/38

[26] For his own declaration of total abstinence ('the pledge'), designed to reduce life assurance premiums, see LRO 3D42/57/155

[27] Malcolm Elliott, 'The Leicester Coffee-House and Cocoa-House Movement', *TLAHS*, Volume 47, 1972

[28] LRO 30D71/21

[29] LRO 3D42/57/41

[30] Marian Emily Ellis married Charles Alfred Cripps (Lord Parmoor) who became a Cabinet member in the first Labour Government in 1924.

[31] LRO 3D42/57/124

[32] *Wrea Head* was eventually given by Edith Ellis, John Edward Ellis's daughter, to the North Riding Education Authority in 1950 and is today a large country hotel. Edith Ellis also gave a large amount of money to start a Charitable Trust.

[33] A.Tilney Bassett, *The Life of John Edward Ellis MP*

[34] Joseph O.Baylen and Norbert J.Gossman (editors), *Biographical Dictionary of Modern British Radicals, Volume 3 1870-1914*

[35] Martin Sharp, 'Two Oadby Benefactors, William E Hutchinson & Rachel Ellis', *Oadby 2000*

[36] LRO DE718/C141

[37] Adam and Charles Back (publisher), *Who Was Who*, 1929-1940

[38] Rita Eaton, *Belgrave: The Beautiful Grove in the Meadows* pp19-27, and for other pieces concerning the sisters

[39] The Mount School, York, also Bootham School, York and Ackworth School, Pontefract are Quaker schools, which are still open.

[40] LRO DE3115/36, 38 and 41

[41] The Leicester Charity Organisation Society was set up in 1876 to co-ordinate local charities. It still runs today under the title of Leicester Charity Link.

[42] Jack Simmons, *Leicester Past and Present*, Volume 2, pp16-19

[43] Names of engines that worked at Barrow-on-Soar were: 3ft-gauge, *Tynemouth*; standard gauge, *Paddy, Flossie, Walton, Charnwood* and *Bridget. Tynemouth* and *Walton* also worked at the Kilby Bridge branch of John Ellis & Sons.

[44] LRO 3D42/57/64

[45] D.A.Ramsey, *Newtown Linford Notes and the Leicestershire Slate Industry*

[46] John & Joseph Ellis Ltd was transferred to Ellis & Everard Ltd in 1963.

[47] Isabel C.Ellis (collected by), *Records of Nineteenth Century Leicester*, p44

[48] There were 11 county representatives on the committee (they included Joseph Ellis of Glenfield, Breedon Everard of Groby and William Everard of Narborough Wood) and 9 representatives of Leicester Borough (including Edward Shipley Ellis). *Leicester Chronicle*, 28 March 1857

[49] Although known as *Sharman's Lodge*, the owners were Rowland and Elizabeth Sherman of Norfolk.

[50] The hall was purchased in 1946 by the Leicester University College and was once the home of Frederick Attenborough (Richard and David's father) who was principal. It is now the residence of the vice-chancellor.

[51] Jack Simmons, 'Mr Colin Ellis', *TLAHS*, Volume 45, 1970

[52] Edward H.Milligan, *Quakers and Railways*, p34

[53] Mary Isabella Legh Ellis, *My Early Life 1904-1931*

[54] *The Wyvern*, 4 December 1891 and 26 January 1901 for general reference

[55] Coincidently, some 60 years later an unrelated hosiery industrialist and county councillor, George Ernest Ellis, owned *Forest Edge* Hence a road serving a small residential estate that eventually replaced the grand eighteenth century house is called Ellis Drive.

[56] LRO Misc161; 12D66/170-180

[57] LRO 8D71/1

[58] LRO 3D42/68/6

[59] J.Newman, *Desford Boys School 1881-1958*

[60] *The Wyvern*, 13 October 1906 for general reference

[61] *The Wyvern*, 15 December 1900 for general reference

[62] LRO DE2031

[63] The sister's niece, Edith Mary Ellis, recalled in 1935 that when they drove to the Leicester Meetings at Soar Lane, the cart was put up at an inn called The Bishop Blaize in Causeway Lane. Carriages from Belgrave Hall and The Gynsills would also arrive at the inn which was used as a rendezvous.

[64] LRO DE3115/73, /77, /87; DE 729/88

[65] Colin D.B.Ellis, *The History of Ellis & Everard Ltd and Joseph Ellis & Sons Ltd* (1924); Colin D.B.Ellis, *Centenary History of Joseph Ellis & Sons Ltd 1839-1939*. Both used for general reference throughout the sector.

[66] Colin D.B.Ellis, *The History of Ellis & Everard Ltd and Joseph Ellis & Sons Ltd* (1924); Colin D.B.Ellis, *The Centenary Book of Ellis & Everard Ltd* (1948); Simon Everard, *Ellis & Everard The First 150 Years (1848-1998)*. All used for general reference throughout the sector.

[67] Leslie Hales and John Pyper (editors), *The 'Old Union' Canals of Leicestershire and Northamptonshire*

[68] Len Noble, *Bardon Hill* pp29, 48 and for general reference

[69] A crusher from 1874 survives at the quarry. It is housed in a large 12-bay building of architectural interest designed by John Breedon Everard. Steps are being taken to preserve machine and building.

[70] LRO L622

[71] Charlotte Ellis, *Sketches of one branch of the Ellis Family in Yorkshire and Leicestershire*, pp16-20; Joan Johnson, *James and Mary Ellis* for general reference

[72] Another brother-in-law, Samuel Priestman, was a director of the Yorkshire & North Midland Railway and then the North Eastern Railway.

[73] David Tregoning and Hugh Cockerell, *Friends for Life, Friends' Provident Life Office*

[74] Because of falling numbers, soon afterwards the rule was changed to allow continuation as a member when 'marrying out' of the religion.

[75] LRO 8D69

[76] *A History of the County of Leicester*, Volume 3, pp2-23 for history of local framework knitting.

BIBLIOGRAPHY AND SOURCES

Ashwell, Dr Ian Y. *John Ellis, Esq., Chairman of the Midland Railway Company*, 2nd edition, 1999*

Back, Adam and Charles (publishers) *Who Was Who, 1929-1940*, 1947

Bassett, A.Tilney *The Life of John Edward Ellis MP*, 1914

Baylen, Joseph O. and Gossman, Norbert J. (editors) *Biographical Dictionary of Modern British Radicals, Volume 3, 1870-1914*, 1988

Beardsmore, J. *The History of Hucknall*, 1909

Bowles, Geoffrey *Knitting Together, Memories of Leicestershire's Hosiery Industry*, 1990

Campton, David *History of Belgrave*, 1927

Clinker, C.R. *The Leicester & Swannington Railway*, 1977

Davies, Hunter *George Stephenson, The remarkable life of the founder of railways*, 1975

Eaton, Rita *Belgrave: The Beautiful Grove in the Meadows*, c.1976*

Ellis, Charlotte *Sketches of One Branch of the Ellis Family in Yorkshire and Leicestershire*, 1870*

Ellis, Colin D.B. *The History of Ellis & Everard Ltd and Joseph Ellis & Sons Ltd*, 1924*

Ellis, Colin D.B. *Centenery History of Joseph Ellis & Sons Ltd 1839-1939*, 1939*

Ellis, Colin D.B. *The Centenery Book of Ellis & Everard Ltd*, 1948*

Ellis, Isabel C. (collected by) *Records of Nineteenth Century Leicester*, 1935*

Ellis, Margaret (compiled by) *Letters and Memorials of Eliza Ellis*, 1883*

Ellis, Mary Isabella Legh *My Early Life 1904-1931*, c.1957*

Ellis, Shirley *A Mill on the Soar*, 1978

Everard, Simon *Ellis & Everard The First 150 Years (1848-1998)*, 1998*

Hales, Leslie and Pyper, John (editors) *The 'Old Union' Canals of Leicestershire and Northamptonshire*, 2nd edition, 1970

Hoskins, W.G. and McKinley, R.A. (editors) *A History of the County of Leicester*, Volume 3, 1955

Johnson, Joan *James and Mary Ellis*, 2000

Mackness, A. M. *Patons & Baldwins Ltd Story of West Bridge Mills Leicester1839-1948*, c.1948*

Milligan, Edward H. *Quakers and Railways*, 1992

Mott, F.T. *Charnwood Forest and Country Lodgings*, 1868

Newman, J. *Desford Boys' School 1881-1958*, c.1959*

Noble, Len *Bardon Hill*, 1995

Ramsey, D.A. *Newtown Linford Notes and the Leicestershire Slate Industry*, 2000

Simmons, Jack *Leicester Past and Present*, Volume 2, 1974

Stenton, Michael and Lees, Stephen *Who's Who of British Members of Parliament*, Volume 1 1832-1885, 1976; Volume 2 1886-1918, 1978

Stretton, Clement E. *The History of the Midland Railway*, 1901

Tregoning, David and Cockerell, Hugh *Friends for Life, Friends' Provident Life Office 1832-1982*, 1982

Williams, Frederick S. *The Midland Railway: its Rise and Progress*, 3rd edition, 1877

Wills, Deryk (editor) *Oadby 2000*, 1999

* Published privately

APPENDIX I   ELLIS FAMILY TREE

All persons shown have the ELLIS surname except those
marrying into the family whose surnames are given. Dates are
shown only for ELLIS family members, though not always
complete.

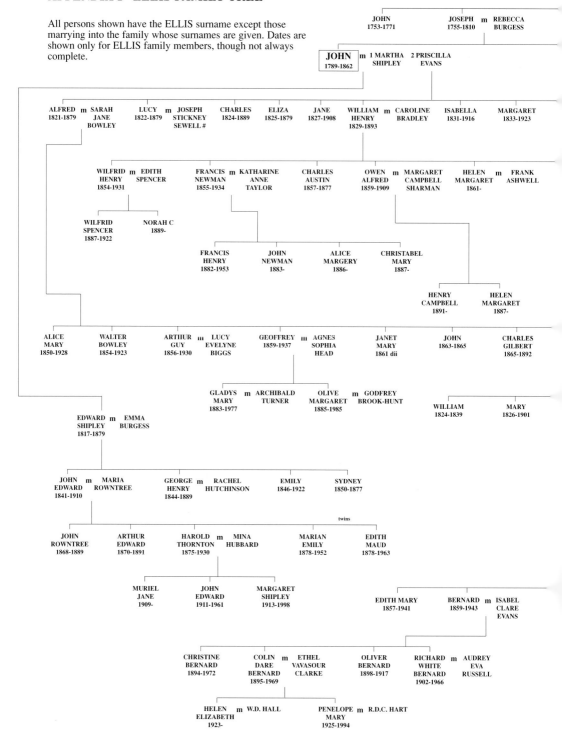

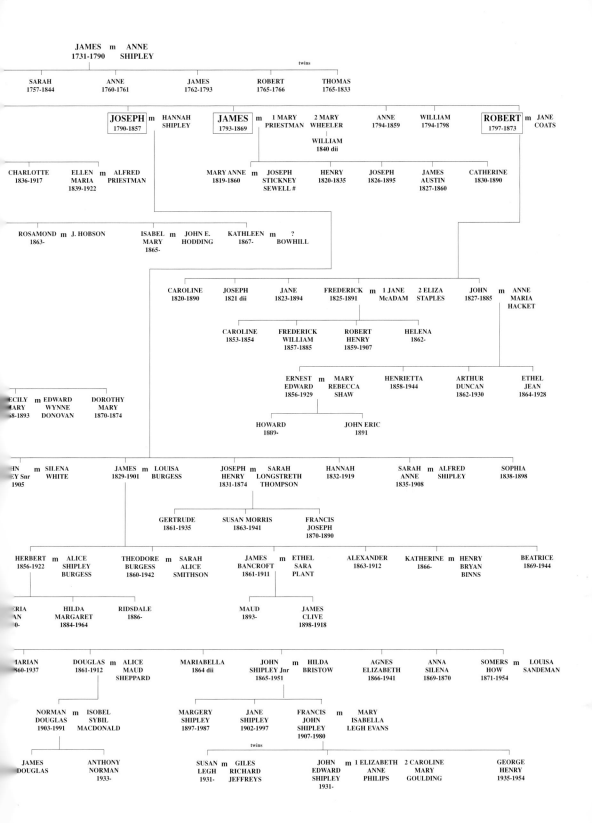

JAMES m ANNE
1731-1790 SHIPLEY

twins

SARAH 1757-1844
ANNE 1760-1761
JAMES 1762-1793
ROBERT 1765-1766
THOMAS 1765-1833

JOSEPH 1790-1857 m HANNAH SHIPLEY
JAMES 1793-1869 m 1 MARY PRIESTMAN 2 MARY WHEELER
WILLIAM 1840 dii
ANNE 1794-1859
WILLIAM 1794-1798
ROBERT 1797-1873 m JANE COATS

CHARLOTTE 1836-1917
ELLEN MARIA 1839-1922 m ALFRED PRIESTMAN
MARY ANNE 1819-1860 m JOSEPH STICKNEY SEWELL #
HENRY 1820-1835
JOSEPH 1826-1895
JAMES AUSTIN 1827-1860
CATHERINE 1830-1890

ROSAMOND 1863- m J. HOBSON
ISABEL MARY 1865- m JOHN E. HODDING
KATHLEEN 1867- m ? BOWHILL

CAROLINE 1820-1890
JOSEPH 1821 dii
JANE 1823-1894
FREDERICK 1825-1891 m 1 JANE McADAM 2 ELIZA STAPLES
JOHN 1827-1885 m ANNE MARIA HACKET

CAROLINE 1853-1854
FREDERICK WILLIAM 1857-1885
ROBERT HENRY 1859-1907
HELENA 1862-

ECILY MARY 68-1893 m EDWARD WYNNE DONOVAN
DOROTHY MARY 1870-1874
ERNEST EDWARD 1856-1929 m MARY REBECCA SHAW
HENRIETTA 1858-1944
ARTHUR DUNCAN 1862-1930
ETHEL JEAN 1864-1928

HOWARD 1889-
JOHN ERIC 1891

HN EY Snr 1905 m SILENA WHITE
JAMES 1829-1901 m LOUISA BURGESS
JOSEPH HENRY 1831-1874 m SARAH LONGSTRETH THOMPSON
HANNAH 1832-1919
SARAH ANNE 1835-1908 m ALFRED SHIPLEY
SOPHIA 1838-1898

GERTRUDE 1861-1935
SUSAN MORRIS 1863-1941
FRANCIS JOSEPH 1870-1890

HERBERT 1856-1922 m ALICE SHIPLEY BURGESS
THEODORE BURGESS 1860-1942 m SARAH ALICE SMITHSON
JAMES BANCROFT 1861-1911 m ETHEL SARA PLANT
ALEXANDER 1863-1912
KATHERINE 1866- m HENRY BRYAN BINNS
BEATRICE 1869-1944

ERIA AN 0-
HILDA MARGARET 1884-1964
RIDSDALE 1886-
MAUD 1893-
JAMES CLIVE 1898-1918

ARIAN 860-1937
DOUGLAS 1861-1912 m ALICE MAUD SHEPPARD
MARIABELLA 1864 dii
JOHN SHIPLEY Jnr 1865-1951 m HILDA BRISTOW
AGNES ELIZABETH 1866-1941
ANNA SILENA 1869-1870
SOMERS HOW 1871-1954 m LOUISA SANDEMAN

NORMAN DOUGLAS 1903-1991 m ISOBEL SYBIL MACDONALD
MARGERY SHIPLEY 1897-1987
JANE SHIPLEY 1902-1997
FRANCIS JOHN SHIPLEY 1907-1980 m MARY ISABELLA LEGH EVANS

twins

JAMES DOUGLAS
ANTHONY NORMAN 1933-
SUSAN LEGH 1931- m GILES RICHARD JEFFREYS
JOHN EDWARD SHIPLEY 1931- m 1 ELIZABETH ANNE PHILIPS 2 CAROLINE MARY GOULDING
GEORGE HENRY 1935-1954

81

APPENDIX II

JOHN ELLIS TESTIMONIAL

The following is an extract from a report of the Midland Railway's General Meeting which was organised to present a testimonial to John Ellis on his retirement from the chairmanship of the company. Written with typical Victorian eloquence, it appeared in the *Leicester Advertiser* on 10 July 1858:

"It will probably be remembered that when the last half-yearly meeting of the Midland Railway proprietors took place, at Derby, it was announced that 1,000 guineas had been voted by the shareholders as a testimonial to John Ellis, Esq., late chairman of the Midland Company. The act of the directors is munificent and proves most potently, and eloquently too, the highest regard for their able, honourable, and universally respected ex-chairman. Few gentlemen deserve honouring more than John Ellis, Esq., frank in heart, unimpeachable in conduct, and of sterling integrity no wonder he has created for himself by the display of such noble qualities real friends and admiring neighbours. There is not on earth a nobler theme for the pen of the journalist than the glorious worth, and splendid life of a truly honest man, whether he be distinguished in local or general society. In speaking of John Ellis, Esq., we feel that we are only rendering that which is due to him even if he were to brighten our praise by having recourse to simile and metaphor. Yet a gentleman with such an enviable reputation for all that is good as Mr. Ellis needs not the aid of the public pen to add lustre to his name, — his deeds form the foundation of his eminence, and the sincere regard of his fellow citizens crowns him with a fame ephemeral and indestructible. Mr. Ellis is remarkable for his business habit and thoroughly practical views, and no doubt his healthful discipline of affairs during his chairmanship tended to elevate the Midland Company and to procure for it wealth and durable distinction.

"It was deemed most appropriate for a portion of the 1,000 guineas to be spent in a portrait of Mr. Ellis and the sum unexpended to be used as the Directors thought proper. We have now to announce that it has been devoted to the purchase of a service of plate, supplied by Messrs. Hunt and Roskell, of London, and which consists of a fine centre piece, which serves also for a candelabrum, two smaller candelabra, four very beautiful dessert-stands, to carry fruit or flowers, two large waiters, a handsome tea set, cake basket, egg frame, two small waiters, and other articles, all of the very finest manufacture. The portrait is by Mr. Lucas, a celebrated artist. Mr. Ellis, we are informed, is represented in a standing position, with his head uncovered, a walking stick in one hand and his hat in the other. The likeness is remarkably accurate. The noticeable characteristics in the features of the original - of firmness and decision, are depicted with fidelity and power. The back-ground and adjuncts are most happily chosen and successfully executed, showing in the distance the single line of the Leicester and Swannington Railway, with which Mr. Ellis's connection with railway matters began. The particular spot selected is the Leicester entrance to the tunnel. This part of the picture was suggested by Mr. Robert Stephenson, as being the scene of his first work as a railway engineer, and by a singular coincidence it happens to be within half a mile of Mr. Ellis's birth-place...

"... On Tuesday evening the directors and principal officials, heads of departments, and personal friends, met at dinner on the occasion of presenting the testimonial, in the shareholder's Room , at the Derby Station, which was decorated in a very tasteful manner with growing plants, flowers, &c. The most attractive feature, however, was the testimonial plate, exhibited on the platform."

The report listed the many distinguished guests at the presentation, although, because of an accident, Robert Stephenson was unable to attend (nor was Sir Joseph Paxton). The unveiling of the portrait and details of the subsequent toasts and glowing tributes in many lengthy speeches were also reported. Two of the speeches were from his sons, Edward Shipley and Alfred, the latter announcing that his father had re-presented the portrait to the directors of the Midland Railway. This, he said, was because, highly as the family would have valued it as an heirloom, they felt more honoured by its being exhibited in the offices of the Midland Railway.

The portrait is now on show at the National Railway Museum, York. On its original inscription (and that accompanying the silverware — pieces of which were eventually bequeathed to John's descendants) were the words: 'Presented by a General Meeting of the Midland Railway Company to JOHN ELLIS, Esq., their Chairman, as a token of their esteem and in grateful recognition of the ability and success with which, for nine years, he has presided over the administration of their affairs, February 18th 1858.' The actual presentation was not until the following 6 July.

From the portrait an engraving was made by Samuel Bellin, copies of which can be seen hung locally in Belgrave Hall museum and at the Home Farm Community Centre, Beaumont Leys.

APPENDIX III

Two extracts from a book of poems, *'Mournful Numbers'* by Colin D.B.Ellis

RUGBY TO PETERBOROUGH LINE
A Song from Bradshaw

By *Rockingham* and *Harborough* the road ran fair and
    wide,
And who would want a better way, to tramp it or to
    ride?
At *Wansford*, heads were shaken then, at *Wakerley* and
    Barrowden,
When first they saw the railwaymen invade the country-
    side.

The turf that fringed the King's highway was broad
    and fresh and green,
And if the road was deep in mud the grass was always
    clean.
—'Twas horrid, at the railway's birth, from *Nassington*
    to *Theddingworth*,
To see the banks of naked earth the metals ran between!

At *Welford*, for the coaching horn, they heard the
    whistling steam,
The couplings clanked in *Castor*, for the clatter of the
    team:
And peasants walking in the dark near *Yelvertoft* and
    Stanford Park,
Would pause upon their way to mark the passing
    engine's gleam.

But now the grass has grown again upon the broken
    ground,
The whistling of the engines is an old, accustomed
    sound;
And down the line, from *Clifton Mill* as far as *Orton
    Waterville*,
Are little country stations still, where quiet can be
    found.

O SWEET CONTENT!

There lives no man that I can see
    Contented in his lot,
But everyone would rather be
    Whatever he is not.
The rich man wishes he were poor,
    The poor that he were rich;
The harassed middle-class are sure
    It would not matter which.

Some men lament that they were born,
    And some that they must die,
And some I see are all forlorn,
    Yet cannot tell me why.
And some who seek for earthly goals
    Find but an earthy grave,
While others strive to save their souls
    Who have no souls to save.

Then leave the world to seek a prize
    That none shall ever find,
And while they weary out their eyes
    Let us be getting blind.
For art is long, but life is short,
    So fill another glass!
And may we never "pass" the port
    While we have port to pass.

APPENDIX IV   LIST OF DEPOTS

The following charts indicate the areas where Joseph Ellis & Sons and Ellis & Everard operated, and the opening dates, where known, of the first depot or retail outlet. The closing dates were not often recorded; the length of time each was open and amount open at any particular time therefore cannot be known. Some depots lasted only a year or two, whereas others remained open for over 100 years. On occasions, some were known to have reopened after closure and some relocated within a town away from the railside.

JOSEPH ELLIS & SONS LTD

DEPOT OR RETAIL OUTLET	COUNTY	APPROX YEAR OPENED	RAILWAY	DEPOT OR RETAIL OUTLET	COUNTY	APPROX YEAR OPENED	RAILWAY
Bagworth	Leics	1851	L&B	Leamington Spa	Warks	1927	~
Barrow-on-Soar	Leics	1898	MCR	Long Buckby	N'thants	1882	NL
Breedon	Leics	?	D&A	Lutterworth	Leics	1898	GCR
Brixworth	N'thants	1920	MH&N	Market Bosworth	Leics	1874	A&N
Broughton Astley	Leics	1890	MCR	Monument Lane, B'ham	Warks	?	BWSV
Burton-on-Trent	Staffs	?	?	Narborough	Leics	1865	S.Leics
Castle Bromwich	Warks	?	W&B	Northfield	Worcs	?	B&G
Coalville	Leics	1881	L&B	Nuneaton	Warks	by 1904	~
Coalville, Ashby Rd	Leics	1935	~	Oadby	Leics	by 1960	~
Countesthorpe	Leics	1840	MCR	Quorn & Woodhouse	Leics	1898	GCR
Coventry	Warks	?	~	Ratby	Leics	1883	L&S
Daventry	N'thants	1889	WDL	Rothley	Leics	1898	GCR
Desford	Leics	by 1860	L&B	Rugby Canal Wharf	Warks	?	~
Elmesthorpe	Leics	1865	S.Leics	Rugby	Warks	1860	MCR
Enderby	Leics	by 1900	~	Rugby, North Street	Warks	1862	~
Forge Mills	Warks	by 1857	W&B	Shackerstone	Leics	?	A&N
Glen Parva Canal Wharf	Leics	1899	~	Shenton	Leics	?	A&N
Glenfield	Leics	1866	L&S	Shepshed	Leics	1924	CFR
Hagley Road, B'ham	Warks	?	HR	Shirley	Warks	1921	B&NW
Hall Green	Worcs	1910	B&NW	South Wigston	Leics	by 1904	MCR
Harborne	Warks	?	HR	Tamworth	Staffs	1857	?
Hathern	Notts	by 1912	MCR	Thurnby	Leics	1899	TL
Highgate Wharf, B'ham	Warks	by 1857	B&G	Ullesthorpe	Leics	1840	MCR
Hinckley	Leics	1873	S.Leics	Water Orton	Warks	1878	W&B
Hinckley, Coventry Rd	Leics	1921	~	Welford & Kilworth	Leics	by 1864	R&S
Kegworth	Notts	by 1912	MCR	Welford Canal Wharf	Leics	1920	~
Kilsby & Crick	N'thants	1882	NL	Welton	N'thants	1878	L&BR
King's Heath	Worcs	by 1855	B&G	West Bridge, Leicester *	Leics	by 1857	L&S
King's Norton	Worcs	1900	B&G	Windsor Street, B'ham	Warks	?	AGB
Kirby Muxloe	Leics	1850	L&B	Yelvertoft & Stanford Pk	N'thants	by 1864	R&S
Lawley Street, B'ham	Warks	?	W&B				

* Also shops at Conduit Street, Wharf Street, St Augustine Street, and Wood Hill

KEY to railways on which depots were situated and pre-grouping (1923) railway operating company (Midland Railway, London & North Western Railway, Great Northern Railway, Great Western Railway, or Great Central Railway).

A&N	Ashby & Nuneaton Joint Railway (LNWR & MR)	LBSCR	London, Brighton & South Coast Railway
AB	Acton Branch (MR & South Western Junc Railway)	L&H	Leicester & Hitchin Railway (MR)
AGB	Aston Goods Branch (LNWR)	L&S	Leicester & Swannington Railway (MR)
B&C	Bedford & Cambridge Railway (MR)	LBL	London & Bedford Line (MR)
B&G	Birmingham & Gloucester Railway (MR)	MCR	Midland Counties Railway (MR)
B&N	Bedford & Northampton Railway (MR)	MH&N	Market Harborough & Northampton Line (LNWR)
B&NW	Birmingham & N. Warwickshire Railway (GWR)	N&P	Northampton & Peterborough Railway (LNWR)
BWSV	B'ham, Wolverhampton & Stour Valley Rly (LNWR)	NL	Northampton Loop (LNWR)
CFR	Charnwood Forest Railway (LNWR)	PW&SB	Peterborough, Wisbech & Sutton Br Rly (M&GNJR)
D&A	Derby & Ashby Branch (MR)	R&S	Rugby & Stamford Branch (LNWR)
GCR	London Extension (GCR)	S&B	Saxby & Bourne Line (MR)
GN	Great Northern Railway Main Line	S&BR	Spalding & Bourne Railway (GNR)
GNL	Great Northern Railway Loop Line	S&P	Syston & Peterborough Railway (MR)
GNLNW	GN & LNW Joint Railway	S&W	Seaton & Wansford Railway (LNWR)
HCL	Hitchin to Cambridge Line (GNR)	SE&C	South Eastern & Chatham Railway
HFB	Higham Ferrers Branch (MR)	S.Leics	South Leicestershire Railway (LNWR)
HL&D	Hertford, Luton & Dunstable Railway (GNR)	SW	Scalford to Waltham Branch (GNR)
HR	Harbourne Railway (LNWR)	TL	Tilton to Leicester Railway (GNR)
K&M	Kettering & Manton Line (MR)	UB	Uppingham Branch (LNWR)
KTH	Kettering, Thrapstone & Huntingdon Railway (MR)	W&B	Whitacre & Birmingham Line (MR)
L&B	Leicester & Burton Line (MR)	WDL	Weedon, Daventry & Leamington Spa Br (LNWR)
L&BR	London & Birmingham Railway (LNWR)		

ELLIS & EVERARD LTD

DEPOT OR RETAIL OUTLET	COUNTY	APPROX YEAR OPENED	RAILWAY	DEPOT OR RETAIL OUTLET	COUNTY	APPROX YEAR OPENED	RAILWAY
Arlesey	Beds	1898	GN	Letchworth	Herts	1915	HCL
Asfordby	Leics	by 1850	S&P	Little Bytham	Lincs	?	GN
Ashby-de-la-Zouch	Leics	1969	~	Littleworth	Lincs	1877	GNL
Ashley & Weston	N'thants	by 1932	R&S	Loughborough	Leics	1964	~
Ashwell	Rutland	by 1851	S&P	Luffenham	Rutland	by 1850	S&P
Baldock	Herts	?	HCL	Manton	Rutland	by 1850	S&P
Battersea (MR Wharf)	Surrey	by 1886	LBSCR	Market Harborough	Leics	1850	R&S
Bedford	Beds	1855	L&H	Medbourne	Leics	by 1932	~
Biggleswade	Beds	1897	GN	Melton Mowbray	Leics	1848	S&P
Blunham	Beds	1880	B&C	Morcott	Rutland	by 1900	R&S
Bourne	Lincs	1866	S&BR	Murrow	Cambs	1866	PW&SB
Brooksby	Leics	by 1851	S&P	Newport Pagnell	Bucks	?	~
Cadwell Sidings	Herts	?	GN	Northampton	N'thants	1930	~
Caldecott/Rockingham	Leics	1850	R&S	Oakham	Rutland	1848	S&P
Cardington	Beds	1857	L&H	Oakley	Beds	1857	L&H
Castle Ashby	N'thants	?	N&P	Olney	Bucks	?	B&N
Clapham Road	Surrey	by 1886	SE&C	Peakirk	N'thants	by 1860	GNL
Clarence Yard	Middx	by 1886	GN	P'borough, Crescent Wharf	N'thants	1848	S&P
Clipston & Oxendon	N'thants	1920	MH&N	Peterborough, GN Yard	N'thants	1882	GN
Cranford	N'thants	1866	KTH	Peterborough, Queen St	N'thants	1900	~
Desborough	N'thants	1920	L&H	Potton	Beds	1913	B&C
Dudding Hill	Middx	1870	AB	Raunds	N'thants	by 1886	KTH
Dunstable	Beds	?	HL&D	Rushden	N'thants	1894	HFB
East Norton	Leics	by 1932	GNLNW	Sandy	Beds	1874	GN
Edmondthorpe & Wymondham	Leics	1893	S&B	Saxby	Leics	by 1851	S&P
Essendine	Rutland	by 1932	GN	Scalford	Leics	?	GNLNW
Eye Green	N'thants	1866	PW&SB	Seaton	Rutland	1850	R&S
Finedon	N'thants	1857	L&H	Sharnbrook	Beds	1857	L&H
Flitwick	Beds	1922	LBL	Shefford	Beds	1857	L&H
Geddington	N'thants	1920	K&M	South Witham	Lincs	1893	S&B
Glendon & Rushton	N'thants	1857	L&H	Southill	Beds	1857	L&H
Great Glen	Leics	1899	L&H	Stamford	Lincs	1848	S&P
Great Easton	Leics	by 1908	~	Stevenage	Herts	1882	GN
Gretton	N'thants	1881	K&M	Tallington	Lincs	1862	GN
Hallaton	Leics	by 1932	GNLNW	Thorney	Cambs	1866	PW&SB
Helpston	N'thants	by 1851	S&P	Tilton	Leics	1880	GNLNW
Henlow	Beds	1857	L&H	Turvey	Beds	1873	B&N
Higham Ferrers	N'thants	1888	HFB	Twywell	N'thants	by 1901	KTH
Hitchin	Herts	1857	GN	Uffington & Barnack	N'thants	by 1851	S&P
Holme	Hunts	1915	GN	Uppingham	Rutland	1895	UB
Irchester	N'thants	1857	L&H	Wakerley	N'thants	1880	S&W
Irthlingborough	N'thants	1920	N&P	Waltham on the Wolds	Leics	by 1925	SW
Isham	N'thants	1857	L&H	Weldon & Corby	N'thants	1881	K&M
John O'Gaunt	Leics	by 1953	GNLNW	Wellingborough	N'thants	1857	L&H
Kettering	N'thants	1857	L&H	West End	Middx	1870	LBL
Ketton	Rutland	by 1855	S&P	Whissendine	Leics	by 1851	S&P
Kibworth	Leics	1899	L&H	Wigston	Leics	1966	~
Lamport	N'thants	1920	MH&N	Willington	Beds	1914	B&C
Leicester, Swan Street	Leics	1966	~	Wisbech	Cambs	1866	PW&SB

LOCATION OF ELLIS & EVERARD BRANCHES AND SUBSIDIARY COMPANIES FOR BUILDING SUPPLIES IN 1974

Bedford	Willow Rd and Greyfriars	Hinckley	Harrowbrook Road	Northampton	Kettering Road North
Biggleswade	Shortmead Street	Hitchin	Wallace Way	Nottingham	Willow Road
Birmingham	Park Road, Hockley	Kettering	Telford Way	Oakham	South Street
Boston	High Street	Leicester	Swan Street	Peterborough	Ivatt Way & Padholme Rd
Bourne	South Street	Loughborough	Station Avenue	Rugby	Somers Road
Coalville	Ashby Road	Mkt Harborough	Clarence Street	Rushden	High Street
Corby		Melton Mowbray	Mill Street	Stamford	Ryhall Road
Coventry	Kingfield Road	Narborough	Station Yard	Stafford	
Dunstable	Eastern Avenue	Newark	Northgate	Wellingborough	Links Road
Glenfield	Mill Lane (Warehouse)	Newcastle u Lyme		Wisbech	Oldfield Lane
Grantham	Harlaxton Road				

BURIAL LOCATIONS

Society of Friends' Burial Ground, Soar Lane

James Ellis 1731-1790
James Ellis 1762-1793
William Ellis 1795-1798
Joseph Ellis 1755-1810
Martha Ellis 1788-1817 (first wife of John Ellis 1789-1862)
Hannah Ellis 1801-1845 (wife of Joseph Ellis 1790-1857)

Belgrave Cemetery

John Shipley Ellis 1828-1905 and wife Silena d.1913
Jane Ellis 1827-1908
Isabella Ellis 1831-1916
Charlotte Ellis 1836-1917
Margaret Ellis 1833-1923

Welford Road Cemetery

Joseph Ellis 1790-1857
John Ellis 1789-1862 and second wife Priscilla d.1872
Robert Ellis 1797-1873
Joseph Henry Ellis 1831-1874 and wife Sarah Longstreth d.1920
Charles Austin Ellis 1857-1877
Sydney Ellis 1850-1877
Eliza Ellis 1825-1879
Edward Shipley Ellis 1817-1879 and wife Emma d.1890
John Ellis 1827-1885 and wife Anne Maria d.1896
Frederick William Ellis 1857-1885
George Henry Ellis 1844-1889 and wife Rachel d.1932
Francis Joseph Ellis 1870-1890
Frederick Ellis 1825-1891 and wife Eliza d.1907
William Henry Ellis 1829-1893 and wife Caroline d.1908
Sophia Ellis 1838-1898
James Ellis 1829-1901 and wife Louisa d.1913
Mary Ellis 1826-1901
James Bancroft Ellis 1861-1911 and wife Ethel Sara d.1945
James Clive Ellis 1898-1918
Hannah Ellis 1832-1919
Emily Ellis 1846-1922
Ernest Edward Ellis 1856-1929
Gertrude Ellis 1861-1935
Theodore Burgess Ellis 1860-1942 and wife Sarah Alice d.1940
Beatrice Ellis 1869-1944

LOCAL MAP OF REFERENCE
Showing main locations and railways mentioned in the text.

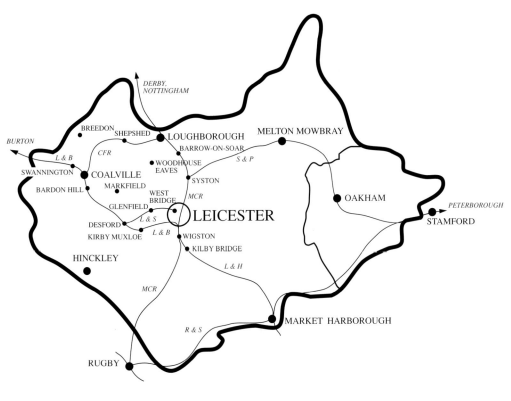

Key

L&S	Leicester & Swannington Railway
MCR	Midland Counties Railway
S&P	Syston & Peterborough Railway
L&B	Leicester & Burton Railway
L&H	Leicester & Hitchin Railway
CFR	Charnwood Forest Railway
R&S	Rugby & Stamford Railway

INDEX

INDEX

INDEX

INDEX

INDEX

INDEX